Editorial

I've long wondered why there is such a virulent separation between popular and 'quality' literature. Envy of success is certainly a factor – *vide* Jack Vettriano in the visual art world, and allied to that the notion so dear to cultural snobs that, by definition, if something is popular it can't be any good *as art*. Yet Iain Crichton Smith devoured detective fiction with a passion (as did that arch-élitist, Yeats). 'Separation' is too mild a word – it is a chasm, and the two camps are looked at as generically different, instead of being embraced under the one umbrella. I have to look into my own breast, and admit to harbouring such prejudices myself in the past. *Chapman* 108 plunges into this great critical divide.

It is of great benefit to Scottish literature as a whole that Messrs Ia(i)ns Banks and Rankin have been so spectacularly successful. William McIlvanney, Irvine Welsh, and even 'the Glasgow school' of Kelman, Gray et al, have all suffered for their success. Here, we attempt to breathe some sense into this contentious area of 'critical metaphysics'.

We are proud to present a fragment from Ian Rankin's forthcoming novel, *The Naming of the Dead*, and an exclusive interview with him. Iain Bank's work is also extensively explored. We look at the younger generation of crime writers, tracing their inspirations back to the likes of Rankin and to McIlvanney, who broke the ground many years ago now. We hope these deliberations will form at least a bridge over the chasm.

Chapman 108 also hosts a wealth of new fiction and poetry. Alan McMunnigal is making a name as an exciting new voice in fiction, and Douglas Thompson's fascinating surrealistic meditation 'Ultrameta' both entrances and perplexes. We have new poetry by Robin Fulton, who committed the cardinal sin of leaving Scotland for Norway and had the cheek (as perceived 30 years ago) to edit *Lines Review* – a *Scottish* literary magazine – from there. I'm also delighed to publish poetry by that maestro of Scotland's Music, John Purser, whose visionary perception of Scotland's cultural wealth has transformed our idea of ourselves. Translation is booming – John Law's masterly translation of 'Alturas de Macchu Picchu' by Neruda shows how powerful and versatile Scots is as a medium. Neil Mac Neil, another *Chapman* regular, is seen here in lively collaboration with Don McNeil, who is also our featured artist. We recommend readers to seek out his Hidden Gallery, deep in mid-Argyll.

Winter Barley by George Gunn is our latest book title. Gunn has achieved recognition (well, some) for his work as a playwright. I hope this book will establish him as an important, indeed major poetic voice.

I apologise for the lateness of this issue: we have encountered many unasked-for problems lately. But our new interactive website is now operational, *Chapman* 109 is nearly ready, and we look forward to reaping benefits from the hard work done by many to develop the magazine.

Neil Mac Neil

Paintings by Don McNeil

Arran from Fintry Bay

Today's shape of time is cold solitude.
January when the sea is neither brash nor loud.
Scotland's fish and saints lie deep, asleep.
But she shines a bright lantern before you, always.
Why you are in this landscape seeking now, puzzles
me. Are you as the sea, sifting through frosted pebbles?

From Fintry you capture Arran's dark, rough granite
ridges, the hopes, treks, the scoured peaks' unuttered fears.
Whatever depth and forms this loneliness may create
it's at least a safe distance from the Witch's Step.
Safe from torn clothes, scraped hands, scuffed knees
from Cir Mhor's slabs of time, black and blue surfaces.

flickering by the frowning headland

flickering beam lights trees   late autumn leaf   winter flame
now a pine fresh breeze moves Eck's blue-grey surface
water   this loch gently laps fallen leaves into garlands on shore
low flying gusts tug your hat   ruffling the headland's eyebrows
tangled arabesque trees drawn in enmeshed stormlight   frown
stealing sun's quanta from November's yellows   russet brown
now harvest reds   glinting watercolour drips from this misty sun
reflect   refract   elliptical troughs between shuwosh   shiwosh
moves of small waves   colours tickling at your loch side boots
in freshwater   rhythmic slaps of brush and light flow into
landscapes   old greens   golds   browns   grey shoulder of cloud
you make brisk strokes splatter forever   this something epiphany.

Warming

Love and hate's scoured peaks. Barely visible snows
blur boundaries between seen, unseen mountains.
Underfoot, new grass puts an end to winter's anthem.
Lightly frozen water whispers about you again
and again. You paint with icy sea water, the new century's
salt on wounds. A landscape of time in Arran's tears.

Today has no taste or colour of mulled wine.
This shape of time, a brush in a jar, frost and sea haze.
Our lives are full of slow speckled thaws, water on paper
or burbling headlong in the glens of Iorsa, of Corsa.
Listen closely, green shoots push up against our ancient heels.
Your scene, as delicate and worn as the Stones of Tormore.

Beside Still Waters Afoam the Sea

This century's first morning rises in a winter haze.
Argyll's cold January landscape sees you no more
than as a pale sun's frown. Or as crimson shadows
among thicket clouds. Your cold palette scatters far.

The north imagines you as Loch Fyne's stilled waters
fallen from winter's dour hooded sky. A new poetry.
Old space, new time (blue-grey in winter light) echo
silent small slow melts. Faint scents, mountain snows.

What you then see brings light and colours, lost shadows
of azaleas on the far shore. In cloud thickets lurking egos
plot. They beckon Spring into their new bothered century.
Under over-fished waters, silent seaweeds, unseen cowries.

Shards

The year our world turned sour we fled
our biggest ever scatter of crowds.
April in Leicester. Where we first heard
the Front spread harsh bleak words

like *us* and *them*. Months before, across the border
something unnamed in me wore gauze thin
layer by layer through Edinburgh's bitter gritter's
strike. A deep freeze in January. In January I fell

into a cone of black light fibrillation.
Stroboscopic scenes. The whole city froze,
unfroze my life in and out of parenthesis.
The worst weather broke into living memory.

My heart grew weak long after dusk.
The bleak white city night held me siren cold.
Wordless, motionless. Unable to pick
out any familiar faces in this suddenly old

light. Later, I told them how I was enticed back
by minstrel ghosts. Chaucer, Dunbar, others. Their lost airs
sounding pibrochs through old bone pipes. How a streak
of cotton-wool mist over well-trekked glens, lifted fears.

Vanished lochs beckoned me. Three blinded pipers
play on high ground. Sunlight on snow
blows back their notes from city to white moors.
Blows back the colour of 'before' to 'after' time.

I told them I thought I'd heard a curlew cry
across the cone of black light. Across winter's
loss of rhythm. Perhaps it was only a longed-for echo
from warm Whin Hill walks of past summers.

Why do memories hide their myths?
As a jaguar in Guatemalan forest?
Corncraiks in the field by Iona Abbey?
Or as weightless chemistries inside the body?

Spring, one year on. In the town *'what's it called?'*
Cherry blossom petals of pink ice spread.
"Are nice," they say. White roses grow wild
up the lattice. In our garden, hope grows cold.

After bursts of blossom, come summer galas.
Brass blows. Flip-flaps of flags and banners.
Yet I still shudder remembering last year.
The hoo-ha. A police 'copter over Leicester

as marchers broke out through the crowd.
Prams fleeing, wailing women trailing men.
Street fright. Street fight. People dive
into shop doorways to avoid. I knew then

we had seen and heard enough to know
we'd all be paid with too much government
more than any of us would need, now, tomorrow,
or in this world's future memory.

People joke that 'THEY' will tax our very air.
To breathe, we'll have to pay for licensed Vader masks.
And, I had no way to know I'd be breathing air in Ratho.
A seventeenth century cold cottage near a low willow.

Today, a late autumn rainbow
veers towards my window.
Over there, deer wander
too close to traffic. Later

at Cramond, skiffs skim water
in the teeth of a northeast wind.
Back home (meaning merely, where I am)
green heaped up piles of rotting boughs

soak mortar off the garden's north wall.
On top of what they call a mulberry tree
a cock crows; One, Two, Three.
Shards hit us all. You. Him. Me.

Our children. What lies before them,
whose Spring had already come covered
in withered fashion's of our love's autumn?
Truth's teetering joys long since departed.

Shards, cargoes of our days. My slate-grey canal narrows
far to the west. Ratho's old legendary stone
ignores a howling dog echo down this village lane.
Tomorrow, it knows. Extremes may come again.

High Wire Act

Mark Gallacher

Widowhood doesn't sit easy with Walter Smith. He says he doesn't understand how I've lived alone these years and been happy. He definitely thinks I'm weird. But I'm the only human being he can call a friend. Frequently Walter finds me infuriating because I never agree things are worse than they used to be. The Estate for example; the way the twin tower blocks are falling apart. Fires in the elevator shafts, unloved children wailing behind pock marked doors, junkie syringes and blood-stained piss sprayed across the concrete stairwells.

What's really bothering Walter is the constant pain in his right hip, his smoker's cough. The whisper of something in his pulse he won't name.

I see him late at night limping past the window of his flat on the 10th floor, directly opposite my tower block. Sometimes he waves, sometimes not. He makes a cup of tea, looks out and smokes another cigarette while the hours fall around him and mournful sirens cross the dark unknowable country below. Sometimes we pretend not to see each other looking back, because even loneliness needs some privacy. If it's a Tuesday he'll point towards the corner of the Estate's car park. Quiz night in The Buccaneer pub.

Walter likes me because I always win something. He knows I read books. He confessed to spying on me once with a pair of binoculars. He saw all the books along the back wall. Hundreds of them, he'll tell anyone with enough whisky to loosen his tongue. And he could clearly see the paintings of the clown, he told me. Just a bit creepy for his taste. And that big black and white photograph of a high wire act. What was that about?

Walter thinks all intellectuals are eccentric in gentle, unthreatening ways. He mistakes my stoicism for wisdom. As if I understand the turnings of the world. Last night in The Buccaneer we won second prize. Six free beers for me and Walter. Walter drank too much. He's a melancholy drunk, prone to ask for reassurance that he's been a good father, a reasonable husband. He thinks he has never amounted to much.

Walter gave me the spare keys to his flat. His daughter in Wales wants him down there again, he explained. She's worried his grandkids won't know him before he's gone. Walter doesn't expect me to go over every night. That's too much of a bother. Just once or twice in the next couple of weeks. Check the post. I told him it would be easier if he just left his kitchen window open. Then I could fly over.

The way I said it made Walter stare at me hard. Then whatever thought held him broke. He stood up, swung to the bar, his bad side limping.

Three days later the Gibson boy appeared on the landing when I had my key in the door. There was some commotion in the lower depths of the stairwell. Shouts. Boots tramped on the concrete steps.

The Gibson boy, already a man in ways I couldn't imagine, ran at me from the stairwell. A hungry nerve-burned lean look, a cruel faraway stare I couldn't fathom. The Gibson brothers were the latest generation to terrorise The Estate. Walter called them Hell's Three Graces. Degradation, Hatred and Misery. But I wasn't thinking that when the Gibson boy pushed me inside my own flat. I could smell fear on his skin. It wasn't the police but something worse on the stairwell. A kind of despair made him reckless.

"Dinnae fuckin breathe," he ordered and grabbed the keys and bolted the door to the flat and dragged me into the living room.

I didn't say a thing and that was a mistake. His gaze flickered round the room and he jabbed a thumb at my portrait. "Whit the fuck is that?"

"It's just a picture. A painting of a clown," I said.

Again his gaze swept across the room, again me. Like radar. He scanned the books. The piano. Reprints of David Robertson's circus photographs along one wall.

"You some sort of perv? Get off on little boy's shorts?"

He dropped a paper bag down on the Rennie Macintosh oval table. What he did next was slam his knife, point end down into the wood. I stepped forward, arms out, ready to reason. He was fast and angry and fell against me like a wall. He battered me around the head with the handle of the knife until I fell to the floor. He looked down where I groaned. I stood back up, more stunned than hurt by the violence.

"Ah'm comin back for this shit tomorrow night," he said and pointed at the bag. "Dinnae let any fucker answer the door. One fuckin gram missing and your shite furniture is chopping board. You along with it. You know who I am. You know my brothers."

He bundled me to the front door and made me open it and look out. "It's clear," I said. "What time tomorrow?"

"What?" he asked amazed and pulled me back.

"I have a hospital appointment," I lied. "Chemotherapy." I wanted to see how suggestible he was. If his brittle will could be bent without breaking into rage. "I'm 73 years old. I'm not too well, son."

He blinked and hesitated. The way I had said 'son', as if it was a kindness. "Tough fuckin titties."

"I might not hear you at the door," I explained. "It makes you sick afterwards."

"Aw. Tha's a fucking shame," he whined. "Ah'll be here at ten."

Then he was gone.

The next day I was nervous but I had time to get to the shops and buy what I needed. On the way back I went over to Walter's. I knew how his flat would be. Spartan. A stale stink of nicotine embedded in the furniture. I raised his kitchen window and latched it open. City noise filtered into the flat and I listened a while and looked across at my own building.

Back at my own flat in the late afternoon I studied the bow and arrows I'd bought in the archery shop. I remembered well how to aim, how to hold it so the tension thrummed along my arm. I tied the string to the arrow and because I knew these events were already pre-ordained, I stepped through the opened patio door onto the tiny balcony and fired the arrow. It sailed into Walter's kitchen on the first shot. There weren't any witnesses. No one looked up any more.

I returned to Walter's flat. The excitement made me breathless. Slowly I pulled the string and the climbing rope came with it. It only took a minute or two until I had the rope in my hand. I made a seizing knot and looped the rope over the taps in Walter's sink at the window, pulled until it was certain the only way the rope could be freed would be to cut it. I returned to my own flat and fastened the rope to the railings of the balcony. The tension was about right. Then I sat down and wrote Walter a goodbye letter.

I told him he was a good man, and shouldn't feel undervalued just because the world didn't listen to him anymore. The value of a man's life was a mystery I wrote, it's coinage memory. I told him he could keep my books. Then, because I felt compelled to, because I thought Walter deserved at least to know something of my past, I wrote the bones of it. Even though the past was so long ago, it felt like someone else's life.

I joined Bendeni's Circus the summer of my sixteenth year in 1947. Practically an orphan my parents didn't miss me. Bendeni the grandfather didn't think me very bright, so he apprenticed me to The Clown, a man called Henderson who beat me if my timing was wrong.

But the grandfather was dead after a year. The son, James Bendeni was kinder. He was the one who'd show me where the bookshops were in every town. He taught me how to balance and four years later I was a part of his high wire act. Everyone in the circus agreed I wasn't a natural, not star material but that wasn't the point. I'd earned my place.

Jimmy wanted me to marry his younger sister Arian, but it was the oldest girl, Beatrice, I loved. Only Beatrice didn't want any man's love and she died of tuberculosis in 1951. Just the circus left to love. Arian married a German lion trainer and they moved to Australia.

Jimmy didn't marry. Began to gamble in his spare time. Cards mostly.

In the winter of 1977, debts and a broken leg, meant Jimmy had to cancel a tour for the first time in the history of Bendeni's Circus. He managed to get most of the others jobs with other circuses around Europe. He loaned the animals out. It was a temporary measure. Everyone sensed it was the end.

I decided to travel. See some of the places I'd only read about. Jimmy made me promise I'd be back for next year's tour. Six months was all I needed I said.

In Puerto Rico I saw the famous high wire artist Karl Wallenda fall to his death. A great silence flew up from the crowd to catch him, but he couldn't be held. I sent Jimmy a postcard telling him I'd decided to travel more. It would be three years before I made it back to Scotland. When I finally came back Jimmy had disappeared. Bendeni's Circus became a footnote in occasional history books on the circus in post-war Britain.

Sometimes I worked in factories, sometimes not. One time a security guard. One time a gardener. I even managed once to work as a lighthouse keeper on Ailsa Craig. That lasted two years. I would climb to the top of the lighthouse and watch the storms drive in from Ireland, see the lightning finger the darkness like Braille.

The money I saved I invested in government bonds and later, stocks and shares. It felt like gambling and I'd think about Jimmy. But I didn't have his bad luck. Eventually there was enough to buy my council flat, a decent pension. A little left over for books and furniture. A life of ordinary, pleasurable things.

After I'd posted the letter I came back to the Estate. The Gibson brothers were in a car in the car park. They were laughing but when they saw me they stopped and watched me go into the tower block.

I'm waiting for the Gibson boy when he finally comes to the door. When I open it he jumps back. I'm dressed in my black circus leotards. Red cape. Bizarre I know but I always preferred the surreal touch. A magic to unnerve. I motion him in with a flick of my long fingers. He's dazed but he follows me into the front room. I talk to him, keeping my voice neutral, just like Arian taught me. My voice tugs at him like an anchor.

"Your stuff is on the table where you left it. I haven't opened it. That's right. There on the table. You should pick it up. Put it in your pocket."

I tell him he is tired and should sit down and he obeys. "Sleep," I say and he closes his eye. "Relax. Deep breaths. That's right."

I go to the balcony. Look down. I can see the car in the car park. Waiting.

I go back to the Gibson boy and tell him when he wakes he will feel relaxed and refreshed. But if he ever touches drugs again he will be sick. If he hears the words hash, smileys, poppers, jellies, crack, speed he will be sick. When he wakes up he will go down to his brothers and give them the paper bag. He will tell them how much he loves them. He will feel loved and happy and relaxed. I tell him to breathe deeply. I count to three and tell him to wake up. The Gibson boy stands up and leaves the flat. In his pocket a bag of pink marshmallows.

I phone the police. Use the local number. I tell them there's a break in. I give my address, my name. Some drug dealers in a frenzy, I say. The Gibson brothers. They mean harm. I'm frightened for my life I say and put the phone down. I walk out onto the balcony and wait. A hot balmy air. The Estate below is dark and gritty. The city proper, meanly lit. Above it all, the night sky glitters softly, awash with blue powdery stars.

I pick up the balancing pole. Drag a chair to the railing and step up. My heart beats fast. Someone swears in the car park. Shouts and outraged curses. A scuffle breaks out among the brothers. "This is a bag of marshmallows Ya fucking numpty."

"Where's the fucking –" "Ah love you. Ah love the two of yous." "Ah'll fuckin do yer heid in. Where's the fucking –" "He's fucking lost it. The auld guy's done something to him" "Listen. Listen tae me. Love is all we need." A great outraged howl roars up from the car park. "Where's the fucking drugs Ya moron?"

There is silence again. Then the sound of retching.

I hear them batter the doors to the tower block. I take my first step out onto the rope. A great singing vibrates in my blood. Years since I felt this alive. Slowly, half step by half step I inch along the rope.

Below in the car park the police arrive, sirens wailing. Lights blink on along the length of the tower blocks. Shouts of amazement begin to ring out around the Estate. More police cars arrive. Then a taxi pulls into the car park and Walter falls out, his upturned face like a small moon. He's come home early.

"Jesus Almighty!" he shouts. "Don't do it, Frank. Your circus days are over!"

That makes me smile and I have to suck a breath of air in to hold my balance. A fire-engine roars into the car park, lights blazing. It couldn't have taken them more than five minutes for all those amazed people to assemble on the car park, like a flock of stunned clowns running around.

I'm a third of the way across. Two shooting stars briefly slice through a dark patch of sky. The Perseids. They are sparks flown from Swift-Tuttle's tail; a celestial firework show winging across the night's big tent.

Strange what I think of, what I remember hanging in the air. I remember how I held my hands out when the great Karl Wallenda fell to his death. But he was too high up, too far away. And like a falling star he made no sound. I remember Beatrice as she smiled and kissed me on the cheek the first time I crossed the wire. If she could love a man, she'd whispered in my ear, then it would be me.

I'm half-way across now. Down on the car park the firemen are inflating some kind of raft to catch my fall. I can only glance down for the briefest of moments.

Then I hear the two older Gibson brothers cursing me from my balcony. The rope wobbles and I have to dip the balancing pole. A great human cry rises from the car park. Some one switches the sirens off. Even the Gibson brothers fall silent. Leave the rope alone.

I've stopped too. My breath almost invisible, my heartbeat still. My mind balanced on its own high wire, between heaven and earth.

Paula Jennings

Autumn Equinox

The Cailleach cannot be stopped.
Patiently she births herself
from the body of the green girl;
my mirror tells me this.
I watch the Old One coming,

wind catching and flapping her rags,
ruffling the feathers of her raven
whose watchful head leans close.
She shuffles through dry leaves
to stand behind my left shoulder

and I hand her the unmarked oval
of my face. Then she smiles
my seasons into me, so implacable
and tender that I want to keep her.
In the mirror I watch her leave,

ankle-deep in the blossoms
of my eighteen year old spring;
but I have her now, in my skin,
in the light patterning of crow's feet,
the steady lines strung between us.

The Menopausal Woman as Several Kinds of Bird

Buzzard

Her hands circle in conversation
while her mind quarters
the ground of memory.

The rodent phrases
take cover,
the cogent facts
are in their burrows.

Puffin

We all know this clown woman
her skin dressed in motley
of hot flush and pallor,
the way her hair won't go right,

the way it clumps out
in gaps and panics,
the jokey bagginess
of hips and thighs,
she looks so surprised,
she must be putting it on
but she can't take it off,
can't take it.

Her heart flaps
like a clockwork bird,
propels her
to a nest of turf on a cliff.
Lulled by the steady suck of sea,
the sun's reliable arc,
the predictable moon,
the clown woman rests
in her stink of fish,
naked in her necklace of puffin beaks.

Albatross

Today the coverlet of water
is shaken in slow motion,
waves bellying
slate-coloured tweed,
weave of quiet light.

At sea she's weightless,
she lets herself be drawn
in vague threadwork.
What is this shape called?
Shearwater? Albatross?

She drifts through the brain's peckings
like a ghost through a wall.

Swan

She's learning to run again
on the surface of the water.
Her black webs beat a flight path
and the great swags of wings
hold tension with such poise
that her hollow bones fill with light.
She's remembering how the whole sky opens
to the white spear of her neck,
how the evening loch rushes to meet her.

A Drinking Woman Explains about the Tiger

The mouth of the bottle is a velvet lover,
kissing my body a new skin;
bullet-proof,
memory-proof.

From the throat of the bottle a voice growls
You are a tiger,
your teeth are switchblades,
your stripes a steel fence.

Then the big cat paces in me,
hot breath and tail-flicking power;
loping plains peel away from my flanks,
my rank scent shouts
Danger
Love me

I burn through high dry grass,
cut you out from the herd.

Imbolc

Bride is in the snowdrops,
inside the green-tipped bells –
and more frost forecast.

The moon sharpens
in a star-shot sky,
and the Crone keens,

rages through branches,
patterns ice-ferns
in her dark kaleidoscope.

First thin light
and here is Bride
crouched among stamens:

petal-skinned February girl
with a knife
in your smile –

slowly you are coiling
the bloodied Crone
back into your womb.

Imbolc: one of the ancient Celtic festivals, 1st February
Bride: Christianised version of the Maiden; Spring aspect of the Triple Goddess.
The Crone: Winter aspect of the Triple Goddess.

A Fine Place

Morag McDowell

Louise has bought a one-bedroom apartment in a desirable part of the commuter belt north of Glasgow because she's reached the age where that's what you do. It's on the top floor and has a balcony where she stood one clear August morning, saw the Campsie Hills spread out on the horizon and calculated there were at least two motorways and a stretch of water between her and Stewart so he couldn't feel unduly crowded. She arranged to move in the third week in September, glad she would have a place of her own to come back to after a bad day at the office, a wide-open, precipitous sanctuary. Now it's November and Louise knows the balcony is in shadow twenty-three hours a day. She knows that plants shrivel and die in the gales that scour the paint off her patio chairs and whistle through the cheap double-glazing. She knows the walls are paper thin. She can hear the people next door and recognise their voices – a man, a woman and a child, a boy. Their bedroom is through the wall from hers. Some nights they fuck noisily to Frank Sinatra singing 'New York, New York'. Some nights they argue. The woman weeps, the man roars like a bull, there are crashes, screams, silences, then Sinatra at full volume. She purchases earplugs, which keep some of it out. When the boy starts whining "Stop it, stop it", in a voice high and reedy with distress, she gets out of bed, wraps herself in her duvet and sits on the balcony, waiting for her hour of sunlight. She meets him in the lift a lot. He seems to wait for her and jumps in just as the doors are closing, already in his school uniform at eight o'clock. He has dusty brown hair that might be blonde in need or a wash and a face that looks like it's just been slapped. She sometimes attempts conversation, but "Hello", "What's your name?" and "Do you like Cartoon Network?" are met with suspicious silence. She starts to take the stairs and calls her solicitor, who says listlessly, "The vendor and surveyors gave no guarantees, Ms McDonald."

When she gets the party invitation from Rhona, she accepts immediately, even though the last time they met was at Rhona's wedding to Joseph in London 18 years ago. She's had letters, which she sometimes answers. She gets chatty phone calls at Christmas and other significant events like the birth of Rhona's daughter and, just after they were married, a postcard saying they'd moved to Helmsdale, a small town on the east coast of Caithness, whose sole points of interest are a nuclear power station and the ferry to Orkney. Louise has been planning to visit anyway – she likes bleak places. She's always reading masochistic travel books – *Greenland – an Odyssey, Bed and Breakfast in the Outer Hebrides* and *Trekking in Eastern Siberia* where she once read 'Ostrov is a fine place to visit but unimaginably remote' and immediately wanted to go there. The party's on a Saturday night. She plans to leave early, take the scenic route, stay over then come back late on the Sunday. She gets up at seven on Saturday morning and tiptoes to the lift. The doors open promptly. She puts her bag down and leans back against the wall, her eyes closed.

"Where are you going?" He's standing in the opposite corner, dressed in a tracksuit and shiny new trainers with red lights in the soles that blink arrhythmically at her as she tries to work out how he's got there. The lift was empty when the doors closed. She's sure.

"Where are you going?"

"Caithness."

"Is that far?"

She nods, tries to place his accent.

"Why?"

"To see a friend. It's her birthday party."

"How old is she?"

"Forty."

"How old are you?"

"Thirty-six."

"I'm ten"

"What's your name?"

"Andrew. I'm from Manchester. I hate it up here. But Mum says we've got to stay with him for a while."

"With whom?"

"Ron"

"Don't you like him?"

He shakes his head and looks away. She starts counting down the floors, wanting to be in the car.

"Will you take me with you?"

She doesn't reply. The lift bell pings. She picks up her bag and walks out to her car.

"Please."

She put her bag into the boot, gets into the driver's seat and starts the engine. She winds down the window.

"I'm sorry Andrew. You'd better go back up."

"I can't."

"Why not?"

He shrugs. "Take me with you."

She feels something inside her drain away, her plan for the day, a slow relaxed drive through forests and glens, past bracken-furred slopes that turn to black rock then disappear into cloud then a stop for lunch somewhere where they serve fresh mussels, a glass of wine, just one.

"Go back up and talk to your Mum. Tell her you want to go home."

He looks at her as though she's stupid. She lets off the handbrake and edges the car forward. He doesn't try to follow her. As she pulls onto the main road, she sees him in the rear view mirror, one hand rubbing an eye the fist scrunched up like a baby's. By the time she's on Great Western Road, her heartbeat has slowed to normal. It's a clear sunny day as she speeds up Loch Lomondside, but she doesn't notice. She's still thinking about him, wondering if she should have taken him back upstairs and waited while he knocked on the door. She switches on the radio.

"And now a report from the Middle East."

She switches it off, imagines him sitting there in the passenger seat beside her, asking, "What's this Rhona like, then?"

"Well, she used to be great fun. We went to university together. She was clever, good-looking. Long black hair, tall and skinny, ate like a horse, always knew the gossip, always last to go home at parties, always sitting there at four in the morning cracking jokes and giving you advice about your life, whether you wanted it or not. We called her the Otago Street Oracle. And a lot of other things besides."

She stops at Fort William for lunch, but can't find fresh mussels so settles for haddock and chips in a pub with tartan wallpaper. She sits at a table in the corner of the lounge watching a television which lurches out from a bracket on the opposite wall beside a menu board advertising Mars bar suppers and haggis *à la cordon bleu*. A news report shows footage of a vast cuboid building with mirrored windows reflecting a blue cloudless sky. One of its walls seems to ripple, a whole side explodes into flames and metal, glass and smoke billow out and down into the street below. The camera lurches and people start to scream. The waitress makes a tut-tutting noise and switches the channel.

She eats quickly and leaves, taking the A82 through the Great Glen then the A9 past Inverness. The landscape flattens out, submitting to the weight of water and sky. She crosses the Dornoch Firth watching them melt together as the sun goes down. The inside of the car is dim and shadowy. She stops on the other side and calls Rhona on her mobile.

"Louise! Natasha's staying with her pal tonight so you can sleep in her room. You're only an hour away, I'll tell Joseph to put the tea on."

The coast road becomes a faint glimmer in the dusk. She follows it over undulating cliffs until the lights of Helmsdale appear below her at the bottom of a long gentle slope. She's been told to stay on the main road, so she follows it down into town past a bar called The Bannockburn, where a man dressed in a football strip is kneeling on the pavement throwing up, then out of town again and round the headland as instructed until she sees a turn-off. Louise has a mental picture of Rhona's house. She's been told it's 'cottage-style' and she imagines one of those white-painted ones you see in tourist posters, with children playing outside, dogs yapping, an Aga in the kitchen and cannabis growing in the vegetable patch. Instead, there's a warren of streets lined with small terraced council houses that wouldn't look out of place in

Easterhouse. There's a rusting Mini in the front garden and, more disturbing, lace curtains in the windows. Just as she gets out of the car, the door opens and a teenage girl with Rhona's dark hair and long pale face runs to the front gate.

"Louise? I'm Natasha. Mum's in the living-room. See you later."

The theme tune to *Eastenders* starts to play tinnily. Natasha takes a mobile phone out of her jeans pocket and walks away talking into it. Louise steps through the front door into the hallway, squinting in the sudden brightness from the bare light-bulb hanging from the ceiling.

"Louise!" Rhona jumps up from an old leather sofa. They embrace then stand back laughing. Rhona's still dark-haired, skinny and good-looking and still talking for Scotland – about Natasha, about Joseph, about the party. Louise can't quite shake off the feeling that she's visiting some place from her distant childhood – there's the coal fire, the TV on a wall-bracket left of the mantelpiece, the table set for dinner facing the wall, and the air warm and heavy with cigarette smoke. Rhona is asking her something and Louise realises she's tuned her out, just as she does when she talks to her on the phone. To her relief, Joseph appears in the doorway.

"Louise." He looks different, older. His face is deeply lined, his hair is grey, long and thick giving him the air of an Old Testament prophet, except that he's wearing an apron and carrying a dish of spaghetti.

"Joseph. That looks good." The fire crackles and spits.

Rhona says, "Let's eat then." The table is set with cutlery, plates, a dish of grated cheese and three glasses of water.

She takes a sip. "I should have bought some wine. Sorry."

Rhona waves the words away with one hand and they eat in silence. The food is good. She remembers vaguely that Joseph might have trained as a chef, before having to give up work. She considers asking him what he's doing now, but tells them instead about the boy in the lift. Rhona is completely unsurprised.

"Kids do strange things. When Natasha was ten, she ran away. Left a note in her room saying not to look for her, that she knew she was adopted and her real parents were descendants of Viking kings and queens. We found her at Duncansby Head, waiting for the ferry to Orkney."

Joseph shook his head. "I wanted to run away when I was a boy. Never felt I belonged in London – knew I'd end up somewhere exotic." He looks ruefully round the room. Rhona laughs merrily on cue then stands up.

"Time to get my glad rags on." She skips out of the room. When Louise has finished her pasta, Joseph goes to the sofa, rolls a cigarette and switches on the television. The sound is turned down, but Louise sees the burnt out shell of the building she saw earlier, photographed from the distance through a telephoto lens, shimmering in a heat haze. She doesn't recognise the city, and is about to ask Joseph to turn the sound up when Rhona re-appears. She's wearing a black T-shirt with a heavy metal logo, black satin trousers with appliqué silver butterflies, leather thong sandals and a green velvet cape. Joseph takes a deep drag on his cigarette.

"Looking good, girl. Looking good."

They walk against the wind round the headland and down into town. At the Bannockburn Bar, the man in the football strip is sitting on the pavement, crying. Joseph walks towards him, nods hello, then heads round the back of the building to a side door. It leads into a small function room, which is hot and smoky and bursting with people. At the far end, an older woman in a black lurex dress is fussing over tables laid with plates of sandwiches and sausages rolls. She turns, sees Rhona and hurries over smiling. Rhona waves.

"That's Mary. Used to be my boss before I gave up work."

Everyone is dressed up, the men in suits and ties or kilts, the women in satin dresses and sparkly shoes with feather boas and bridesmaid hair with diamanté clips, all slightly drunk and chattering. Apart from Louise, the only other person in jeans is Natasha, who drifts over from the bar towards her mother. Rhona is surrounded by people. They hand her presents, she smiles benignly, opens them then passes them back regally to Natasha. Louise buys some drinks and finds a table. A group of young girls wearing silver-blue eye-shadow, halter-tops and cowboy boots start to do a pre-rehearsed dance routine in the middle of the floor. The crowd cheers and claps. Rhona comes over and sits down, flushed and grinning. Louise looks at her in mock appraisal.

"Popular as always."

"I was worried that no-one would come. How's the new flat?"

"OK. Apart from my neighbours."

"Ah. The boy in the lift."

Louise nods. Rhona leans over and says in her ear. "Joseph's given it up."

"Given what up?"

"What do you think?" Louise looks up to where Joseph is standing on his own hugging a can of Diet Coke.

"Good. Has he – given it up before?"

"Lots of times."

"What if he starts again?"

"I'll get stoned, take a boat to Stromness and find myself an Orcadian chambered cairn to lie in," Louise says dryly.

"As long as you're happy"

"I am tonight."

"So what do you think I should do about him?"

"Who?"

"The boy in the lift." She blows out a plume of smoke and watches it curl slowly up towards the ceiling. "Forget the boy. Find yourself a man."

"I've got one."

"Where is he then?"

"At a conference in Prague."

"Am I supposed to be impressed?" She winks. "Only joking. Let's dance. We'll sort out your life in the morning." She jumps up and weaves into the crowd using the same rock-chick belly-dance movement that Louise remembers from twenty years ago. Somehow it still works. When the pub manager throws them out at two, the party continues in Rhona's living room Louise stays up dutifully drinking whisky and Irn Bru. At four she says goodnight, climbs the stairs to Natasha's room. There's something hard under the pillow of the single bed. She reaches in and pulls out a diary. As she puts it on the floor, it falls open at today's entry.

> Mum's Birthday hope she doesn't start dancing, hope Jo drinks Diet Coke hope London calls they said they would if they don't I'll go anyway I'm out of here if it's the Wick coach, a rapist's car or a sheep truck I don't fucking care and God please don't make her wear the green cloak tonight

She closes the diary, and falls into a deep sleep.

It's still dark outside, when she starts awake a few hours later. She makes herself toast then goes to the car, thinking she'll call Rhona later and explain. She takes the quick way back via Stirling and is home by noon. She almost throws up in the lift, but it's passed by the time she reaches the 20th floor. All she wants to do is sleep, but she needs to find out about the boy. She walks to her neighbour's door and presses the bell. There is a long silence, then footsteps, the door opens and the man she assumes must be Ron is standing there, barefoot. He's small, with dark hair, a fine-boned face blurred with sleep and a soft feminine mouth. She tries to imagine the bellowing voice she hears through her bedroom wall, then wonders what she expected – a string vest and tattoos?

"Hi. We're neighbours."

He looks at her blankly.

"I was wondering if Andrew was OK."

"Andrew?"

"Yes. Andrew. The boy."

For a moment she wonders if she's imagined it all, but then he says, "They don't live here any more."

He starts to close the door, but she leans into it.

"Where have they gone?"

"South. Back down South." He says it too quickly. His eyes waken up as he speaks, meeting her gaze, holding it, not letting go until she smiles.

"Right. Sorry to have disturbed you."

The door shuts before she's finished speaking. She goes into her flat, drops her bag, walks through the hallway and living-room and steps out onto the balcony. The wind tickles and moans around her ears. She sits down with her coat still on and watches the storm clouds boiling in.

Clare Crossman

Island
(after Islay)

The island will take you and wrap you in a might of weather:
smoke and honey you in the brown of p eat,
batter your house with Atlantic storms.
When the rain comes, all the daisy petals fall,
marigolds in the garden, dissolving to topaz
pollen melting to a thin golden dust.

The white houses rowed on the harbour front
brace, to out-fence the gale. Water will cool you,
beyond the cities' reach: starfall and coast guard,
fish-haul, the cut of the light house beam.
On hot afternoons, you will lie in the first burn
you come to, under an arch of ferns.

Iron boats bought you here and are the only
road back.The skylight covered in water beads,
thrift and swallows reaching for the eaves.
You are bound in like a hermit
perhaps because of the journey,
the strange music of seal howl on
the last stretch of land.

Let time go, let the square clock tick,
scribble colours in a book of hours.
The sea returns everything in its own image:
plastic smoothed to malachite and quartz,
wrenched floats lichened on turquoise rope.

The ocean holding no patience with the ways
in which we try to destroy ourselves,
the tide its only love: the deep silence,
the continual waves embrace.

The Golden Journey

Re-reading them, I am taken back there,
to the first house I remember.
Square rooms, my bedroom window that
looked out across the town. Our fingerprints
in dust on the banisters to the attic where the
skylight collected water-beads and stars.

The night light burning down,
thick blankets kept winter out.
Under the covers with a torch, the
starched sheets, a warm hollow for my
breathing and my books where phrases
were like music singing a simple world.

I wonder if I seem as wrinkled now
as those relations who arrived in
shiny shoes, with permed or backcombed hair.
Sinewed and powdered they looked like
ancient horses from a fairy tale, we had
learned at school.

I think of it as recent that I was
given those books: heavy paper, gifts
of pattern, celebration to wonder at on rainy
afternoons. Love encircling me
with what I half already knew,
that I was solitary, preferred to
stand outside, watching from a distance.

We never lose what happens
when we are only in the present.
Existing in minutes, seconds, each
day a chance to reach for who we are.
Those rooms forever open in our minds,
when we knew no paths beyond the gate,
and did not see how dark can extinguish light,

or that we could be so old and tall.

Kin

You say you always lived in books,
driving one battered car across a desert,
spending nights alone in motels,
beside the shadow of hibiscus on the wall.
The way words are: describing romances,
betrayals, ordinary things. The shimmer
of those things which make us human:
the ways we learn to live with who we are.

You remind me of other people I have known:
who lived to understand a phrase in music,
lift carmine on a brush, translate
what's difficult into the fall of light,
certain of the need for elegance.

We meet in cafés, talk against
the coffee makers hiss, under
a mirrors glare.

Smoke curls and falls into a winter afternoon,
and there is no need to explain how,
certain chords can catch the heart,
the way blue slips to grey, when starlings
row along the eaves. There is a gathering in.
Outside in the street, leaves pile to markers,
like tracings on the maps of love,
the rustle of pages, under the skylights
of other high up attic rooms.

The Pendant

Green glass stone of the place
I come from, where the wind is
always present, buffeting hill towns.
In crowded rooms, you hold the
glow of faces on the surface of your pool.
Around my neck, your shape is
caught in a silver circle, crafted

under a single light where people
wear the sky like a coat, weather begins
in clouds and there is no escaping
the certainty of stars, the first salt of frost.
In the city you catch headlights, the
leaves pattern on the pavement,
stark avenues of black trees.

Like the blankets of street dwellers
and their long braids: talisman of another
tribe, an invisible thread to the
whispering of land, the certainty of stone.
What do others wear close to their
hearts. Where everywhere is home
and there is so much separation?

In the blur of days, on neon pavements
Perhaps a folded letter, a locket with
two faces always in a kiss.
A heaviness, thumbed kept close,
a map, inscribed with memory, held fast,
imprinted with where we travelled from
small paper lanterns, amongst enormous moons.

Fiddle-fish and Wave at Kettles Yard
(Jim Ede founded Kettles Yard, Cambridge in 1956)

They came to him the man who kept the light,
the *tesserae* of coasts, the shells and rocks,
the smoothed wood and the stones.
They brought letters printed on cloth,
boats from a children's storybook,
the stern lines of winter trees, the holiness of flowers.
It was easy. There was no contradiction between
the waves arc, the fall of clay, marble on a rope
moving like the liquid silver scales of a fish,
everything had a rhythm and a flight.

He collected sculpture, paintings to settle
on the plain surfaces of his house,
amongst the smell of cooking, the turn of pages,
slate and the creaking of stairs.
Underneath the surface: a basic shape of bone,
outlines of legs and face, arms to reach, cradle or kill,
celebrate and dance, hold up the air.
As well to be émigré, in a pair of worn out shoes.

He knew those artists from his journeys,
on trains and planes, amongst all shades of colour,
east and west. Reaching to touch those things,
which make us human: a naked eye the edge of the world,
believing in the power of dreams.
What better than to open windows, treasure glass,
leave us with a question about stars?

Every day they echo, what he left with cornflowers:
an image of their fragile blue and the suns' blazing.
The essence of what we half already know:
these surfaces of oil, copper scraped to make
the outlines of a cat, the glint of horses heads,
details of wings. Everything sacred to the ground,
and God with many names.

Cartography

An old map shows how the field was once hedged
and strips of land planted with orchards,
before they grew wild. Perhaps this accounts for
the feeling of Eden, branches of hazel and elder
left where they fall.

I never see them, the others who come here.
They have bridged the ditch with a plank,
made a fire in the clearing put a circle of
stones under the chestnut tree.

I wonder if they stay out all night
watching for foxes while the moon is outlined
by the ash, and Pegasus' wings are drawn
in punched stars. They leave no trace,
except for places where they have lain in the grass.

I know they have been there: a thread of cotton
on a stick, an empty tin, marks this rough ground.
We share the same knowledge
of earth on our skin, the solace of trees,
perhaps an unblinking stare.
Like the deer who cross, these woods every morning
in the first unfolding light.

The Card You Sent
(After The Picnic Party by Jack Vettriano)

That's you in front with an umbrella,
and me behind with a straw picnic basket.
My husband holds an open parasol against
the breeze, that is pushing us in the opposite
direction from where we are trying to go.
In our summer dresses, mine with gold spots
and yours with pink, his red banded straw hat,
and barefoot, we are mirrored on wet sand.

You are balancing yourself with your free hand,
like the girl you still believe you are at forty-three.
And we have set out on this watery day,
to walk to the cove we imagine at the end of the strand.
Three old friends traversing a beach,
trying to save each other, from that
private darkness that turns the tide too quickly for you.

We'll gaze along the shoreline, eat our picnic,
lie in the long grass, listen to the tide. Until
everything dissolves to watercolour,
a smoke of ochre, ivory and blue.
It seeming for a moment to be easy
to put the world right and hold it there,
like this painting, on the card you sent.

Ian Rankin Interviewed

Edmund O'Connor

"Rankin and Rebus: Bestsellers", reads the publisher's blurb. For once, there's no hype. Ian Rankin is possibly the most successful modern Scottish male novelist with his novels on Inspector Rebus of Lothian & Borders Police. Though born in Fife, Rankin has become synonymous with Edinburgh through Rebus. Weaving together elements from wide-ranging sources such as R L Stevenson, James Hogg and James Ellroy, Rankin has made Rebus and his adventures a unique presence in Scottish writing. Yet despite this success, and the clear influence Scotland has had on Rankin, critical debate has been muted, with only occasional mentions of his work now being made nearly 20 years after he started writing.

Edmund O'Connor: *You've said that when you wrote* Knots and Crosses *you wanted to write a 'proper' novel that was taken seriously by academics. Did those factors influence you when you started writing?*

Ian Rankin: Not to begin with. I started writing aged seven or eight. But having gone through undergraduate English literature and then starting a postgraduate degree, I got sucked into the 'literati' machine. There was this split, a psychosis in me – half wanting to be a self-supporting, populist writer and the other half wanting a pat on the head from the university professors. I'd already had the example of Umberto Eco with *The Name of the Rose*, which was a take on the classic detective novel.

I put a little extra spin on *Knots and Crosses* by doing a twist on *Jekyll and Hyde*, formed as a detective novel. Not that every chapter is a mirror image of it, but that novel reverberated in my head as I was creating the relationship between the two. They were blood brothers at one point and then one becomes a villain out to destroy the other. The 'villain' is maybe not your evil half, but the half of you that's driven by unbridled passions and emotions will try to destroy the reasoning half.

EO'C: *You said when you started you were driven partly by a need to 'please' academia but you don't care as much now. When did the change take place?*

IR: It changed quite quickly. When I started reading crime fiction I found lots of good things in it – and bad things too – but then there are lots of bad things in literary fiction. I thought: "Crime fiction's doing OK on its own and if professors want to come along and say this stuff's valid that's fine but we shouldn't go out of our way to make it more acceptable to them." Crime writers should be writing the books they want to write, not the kind of books they think a small section of the public want.

My main concern was to write books about contemporary Scotland and, with each book to say something about a new bit of the puzzle – the oil industry, the legal system, the political system or whatever. We've got people like Gill Plain writing a scholarly book about *Black and Blue*; I've got honorary doctorates from a couple of universities, the books are studied in schools in Scotland, some in universities abroad. So it has happened – I just bided my time and waited for academia to come to me.

EO'C: *Do you think that crime fiction is seen by many people as a 'lesser' form of novel – it has to achieve something 'extra-special' to be considered seriously?*

IR: There is a weird rule, a law of nature that if a crime novel is good and breaks the boundaries, suddenly it's not a crime novel any more. *Miss Smila's Feeling for Snow* is not a crime novel because it supposedly does more than a traditional crime novel. Same with Dostoevsky's *Crime and Punishment*. It's more a case, to be brutally frank, of how publishers pitch the book. If a publisher puts a certain kind of jacket on a book and its sales -force tell bookshops certain things then they think that's what the book is. If they say "Well, it's not a straightforward whodunit, it's a searing literary *exposé* of the state of the nation" then you brand it in a different way.

In universities, they're starting to study crime fiction alongside other kinds of fiction, giving it a respectability it hasn't had before. So we do depend on scholars and teachers to say look, this *is* actually worth reading, not just something you buy at an airport then chuck away. Often, there are layers you won't get on first reading. If you're just looking for the puzzle element, which there is in all crime fiction, then you'll miss out on a lot. In fact the puzzle element is the least satisfactory part. I hate having to put in red herrings to mislead the reader – I'd like just to tell them at the start exactly what's happening so we can get on and tell the real story.

EO'C: *Gill Plain says that while crime fiction has been 'accepted', the real break-through will be when a crime novel is short-listed for a major literary prize …*

IR: Sure. That's difficult for crime writers like P D James or Ruth Rendell who are writing brilliant books. Brilliant crime novels find it hard to get on to the Booker short-list just because of their name. If a new young writer comes along, then it's more likely, perhaps. It's happened with John Williams who's on World Book Day's list of top ten books that say something about the world we live in. In Scotland, *Set in Darkness* is in the top ten. In Wales, Williams' novel *Cardiff Dead* made it on to the list as well. But in England, it's the same old usual suspects – Zadie Smith etc. No English crime novels are on the list. Maybe it's a peculiarly English thing because when people think of the crime novel they think of Agatha Christie and Dorothy L Sayers. We don't have that tradition in Scotland or Wales, so maybe we don't have that monkey on our back.

EO'C: *So you only see crime fiction being taken seriously only up to a point?*

IR: If the literary establishment decides it's no longer a crime novel or it goes on the Booker short-list then it's no longer a crime novel, it's contemporary fiction. All these barriers and boundaries have been put up without thought. It's hard to justify why one book goes into the science fiction section or the fantasy section and not into the literary or straight fiction section. Why are some books in the fiction section and not the crime section? It's bookshops being told what the book is.

EO'C: *Gill Plain also states that the crime novel is a powerful vehicles for social criticism. How far do you see your books as social criticism, commentary ...?*

IR: There's always a theme of society in flux, society in crisis in the books. Crime, by its very nature, is a sign that society isn't working. If we lived in a perfect world, we wouldn't have people who felt the need to commit crimes and crime would disappear over-night. But we know from Adam and Eve, there's no such thing as a perfect world. That flaw is within us from the start, it's part of our nature and that makes crime fiction serious fiction. It can investigate areas the literary novel doesn't go into because it's too concerned with being 'literary'. I can't imagine Fay Weldon trying it, Alain de Botton or somebody, having a go at terrorism.

There's always been in my books an element of trying to find out what makes Scotland tick and as soon as you look at crime you start asking why people commit crimes and you do come to social conclusions. It's to do with where they've been born and brought up, the family, and the lessons they've learnt as kids. Sometimes it's a lack of social awareness.

Edinburgh's a fascinating place to write about because it has this split between the rich and the very poor. The tourist never sees the pockets of deprivation. When I first started writing the books I was very conscious of the Edinburgh the tourists saw, and the Edinburgh most of us actually lived in. As a student I lived in some pretty rough areas – on the edges of Craigmillar in my first year. Walking into town to the university, I was conscious of almost walking through 'ripples' – towards the centre the place gets nicer and nicer and suddenly you see more tourists. You realise the city they see is a mask the real city is wearing, saying "Please look at Greyfriars Bobby, take your photograph and get back on the bus"; "Don't hang around, don't investigate" and what was just beneath the surface in the '80s was crime, poverty, drug problems, HIV and the rest. I couldn't see a way of writing about Edinburgh without bringing that in. The two cities do seem to reflect the *Jekyll and Hyde* nature of human experience.

EO'C: *Val McDermid has said that recently, crime fiction has a lot more to say about society than literary fiction. Is this a recent development?*

IR: I don't know if it's a recent development but the crime fiction we know about from the past tends to be the stuff that's lasted – it has this view of a society that has never existed, really, a village England. Into this ideal of English life we suddenly have this eruption of violence, the *status quo* gets interrupted and then you need intelligent, right-minded people, usually upper or upper-middle classes, not professional police officers, but amateurs, to come in to solve the crime and make everything right again. It's like a Shakespearean comedy where everything's been shaken up but in the end it's OK. Then your amateur detective goes off to another village in the next book and the same thing happens. They have no self-awareness, the crimes they investigate never change them and they don't think to themselves, "How come everywhere I go a murder happens?" It's as though murder doesn't change – the books are hermetically sealed.

What we get now in crime fiction is a more urban novel looking at urban experience, in which the good guys and the bad guys aren't black and white – it's hard to separate them. Good guys may have a dark moral centre and the bad guys may even have redeeming qualities. So there's a lot of grey people out there. And you can't have a happy conclusion – if a murder happens, even if the person is sentenced and put away, there's still a gap in the world where that person used to be. So there's a greater sense that the world gets shaken up and the *status quo* never resumes.

EO'C: *Do you think that the serial nature of your books – one overarching story with several chapters instead of several separate stories – is problematic?*

IR: The series is meant to comprise a jigsaw so only if you read the books all the way through will you actually get a whole picture. You're getting different aspects of Rebus's character and different aspects of other characters from the books, learning more about them, things you didn't know in book 1 as you go on. So what do you do about the reader who comes in at book 13? How much back story do you give? How much can you explain these characters without boring the regular readers who've been with you since book 1? That's problematic when you're doing a series, which is why so few people do it.

But the real strength for me is you do get that sense of the world changing and of characters changing, the world affecting them. What you often get in crime fiction that isn't serially driven is the same writer creating different characters but in very similar situations in different books. The characters seem very similar and they all blur into one anyway without you getting that sense of one person changing through time.

EO'C: *So does a serial author get to know his characters more closely, know every single aspect about them, see where they want to take them …?*

IR: No. I don't know what I'm going to say about Rebus at first. It's only when I start a new book, do I think: "How would he react to this? Has he dealt with this before? Is there something in his past that could be useful for this investigation? Are there things about him I don't know that could be useful here?" And I start to add layers to his character. In the one I've just finished, he's in an investigation involving someone who's been in the SAS, come out of the army and gone a bit berserk. Well, Rebus himself doesn't fit into polite society, but he also has an army background and so he's brought in to say, is there anything you can tell us about this character? There's no mystery – the opening sentence is: "There's no mystery". We know what this guy did and he's dead now so there's no whodunnit element to it – the only question is why did he do it? So Rebus has to answer that – a much more interesting question: the 'whydunnit'.

I think don't think about it in advance and decide what I'm going to say. Some writers are horrified at the idea that you make a book up as you go along. But many crime writers work that way. James Ellroy knows every single thing that's going to happen, plots it out in insane detail; 2-300 page synopses – but P D James, whose books are very carefully and classically structured, says she starts at the beginning and sees how things pan out. You can't start to work out the moral dilemmas the characters may be in until you get to know them. Every time I meet a crime writer I ask: when you start a book, do you know how it's going to turn out?

EO'C: *You've clearly enjoyed working with the character of Rebus. Do you think there are limits to where you can take him and the series?*

IR: There are limitations to what you can do. Having invented a series set in contemporary Edinburgh with a cynical, middle-aged cop I can't suddenly think, "I'd love to write a comedy". In one book, *The Hanging Garden*, about a war crime from World War II in France, I struggled for ages to think how to contain that in a modern Edinburgh novel. I got an idea for a story and then had to work at incorporating it into the setting.

There will come a time when I'll have nothing new to say or find out about Rebus, and that's when the series ends. But he also lives in real time so there are only a certain number of books to go before he reaches retirement age. One reason for stopping would be if I got an idea – a theme I want to explore – that couldn't be contained there. That's usually what happens first: then I think, "OK, how could Rebus tackle this? How can I use him to ask these questions or investigate this theme?" If a theme came along I couldn't use him for, I'd have to write a different book. Hasn't happened yet. I've promised myself to read the series from the beginning and see if I need to write any more or is it self-contained and as good as it's going to get? And is there anything else I want to write?

E'OC: *Can you see an academic career appealing? Creative writing perhaps?*

IR: I don't think you can teach creative writing, so I've got no interest in that. If people have got talent you can show which direction to take it in. If people have no talent, you can't turn them into writers, which a lot of these creative writing courses pretend they can. But, when I was at Edinburgh University I did get a lot out of the Writers in Residence who came in one day a week. You got to hand stuff over to them – poems, plays, whatever, and then the next week you'd get it back and have a one-to-one session. One year it happened to be Allan Massie – a relief to me because he was a novelist and he was a huge influence early on. Not only in making me think I could be a writer but also the kinds of things I was writing. When I wrote *Knots and Crosses* and it became a crime novel I wrote to him, said, "Sorry, I've written a crime novel". He said, "Look, John Buchan wrote great crime novels and nobody looks down at him". He was very positive about the whole idea, not thinking it a stigma if you're a genre writer as long as you're writing what you want to write.

E O'C: *You say you remember sitting in a tutorial on* The Flood *incognito and being quietly amazed about what people were saying about it. And you posed the question: Can the book be cleverer than the author?*

IR: I think my books are cleverer than the author. When I was doing postgraduate research I came to believe in 'reader response criticism': that whatever the reader thinks is in the book *is* in the book. What you take out obviously is in there for you, but the author may not have put it there. Cairns Craig was teaching this tutorial to first year Scottish Literature students and asked me to sit in and they didn't know who I was. I sat there quietly and an American guy read out his essay. He had *Wasteland* imagery, colour images, the four elements, and all the rest of it. I was scribbling it all down, I thought this was brilliant. I didn't remember structuring it that way. He was bringing out structures which, if they were there at all, was either by accident or at a subconscious level – you're not always conscious of themes and meeting-points between themes.

People make connections, and you think, "Yeah, that's right." I did this in a gauche way to Alasdair Gray when *1982, Janine* appeared, he came to do a talk. Afterwards we went to the pub and I said, "the book reminds me a lot of *A Drunk Man Looks at a Thistle*. A hundred people must have told him that but he said, "Oooh, you're right, it's probably an influence I wasn't aware of". He got a real buzz out the fact that you thought you'd seen something in the book that he wasn't aware of himself.

EO'C: *So there's two people writing: the conscious and unconscious author?*

IR: There are three authors: the conscious author, the unconscious author and the accidental author. The accidental author writes things that have no connection at all except in the mind of one reader, somewhere. If that reader sees it, it's obviously there. I get emails and letters from readers, finding things I wasn't consciously aware of – half lines from songs: "Oh, Rebus has this line – and it's a line from a song", and you think: "Well, I don't have that album, don't remember that band but maybe I heard it on the radio and it lay there in my unsubconscious until needed for something Rebus could usefully say. I love 'the aleatory', 'the accidental nature of creation', not going as far as Burroughs and using cut-up techniques. But there's a lot of serendipity involved. – You've got one story and another subplot and then suddenly see where the subplot could connect to the main plot to make a more fulfilling read. Some characters only enter the book because you need someone to fill in a scene in a pub and you suddenly say, "Hey, this could be the guy who did X to Y, so Z's after him". That's great when it starts to happen.

EO'C: *You said Siobhan Clarke was an accidental creation but she's assumed a larger role in recent novels. So you can take a character you dreamed up, introduce them, and make them a more substantial character than they were.*

IR: She was meant to be a very minor character, as was Cafferty, the main villain, but was just too interesting. I thought, "I don't want to let you go, for you to come in now and again and say, 'Yes sir, I'll go and do that for you, sir'" I created a character with lots of tensions within her. She's English with a Gaelic name, a woman in what's still seen as a man's profession, a Hibs fan in what is still a kind of Hearts-driven sphere.

Lots of things make Siobhan interesting. She's attracted to Rebus's way of doing things, but is also canny and wants to move up the ranks – she's just on the side of the angels, and no more. Same with Cafferty. He was meant just to be a stereotypical villain who runs Edinburgh, but there was a lot I could say about Rebus through him: they've similar ways of looking at the world: one has chosen one route and one has chosen the other, and yet at any point they may destroy each other.

E O'C: *I've been tempted to read into the Rebus/Cafferty relationship echoes of Holmes and Moriarty.*

IR: Rebus in the early books doesn't have a partner because I thought he didn't need one, but then I thought, "Wait! In crime fiction you've got to have a partner". So I created Brian Holmes – then thought I didn't need him. Rebus should be like King Lear, a man alone on the heath raging against the world. So I strip away his friends, put his daughter in a wheelchair, send her down to England and have his wife leave him. I get rid of social encumberances so he becomes 'the man alone'.

By then I had Siobhan Clarke in for Holmes to interact with. She was much further down the food chain but just resolutely dug in and said, "I'm not leaving these books, I want to stay here."

EO'C: *You've said you were toying with retiring Rebus and having Siobhan take over. Wouldn't that be the triumph of the accidental over the conscious?*

IR: It would be a triumph of aleatory art. There's that kneejerk idea that men can't write well about women. Women can write well about men but not men about women, *especially* in the crime genre. We think nothing of P D James or Ruth Rendell having male characters as their protagonists but with a male crime writer and a female heroine it becomes much tougher to be recognised for doing it well. So that's why I held off.

People like Jill Templer (Rebus's boss and ex-lover) don't appear much in early books because I didn't feel confident. But when crime writers like Val McDermid, or women cops, said, "I like what you do with Jill (or Siobhan)", I felt OK to do more with them. I'm still not sure. There are two constituencies: people who won't accept a man writing from a woman's point of view, and Rebus fans who won't accept he's not there any more. They don't want Siobhan to be the hero of the books, they want Rebus.

EO'C: *You didn't want to fall into the trap McIlvanney falls into with Laidlaw in portraying women – as the whore, the mother or the shrew ...*

IR: That's there too in the Rebus books – something in the genre makes people take certain roles. In the early books, there were deceitful women. But you could say the same about heroines in Ellroy's fiction or the American crime novel. It's tough to get away from. I've done it with Siobhan because she isn't a stereotype. She's confused, doesn't always do the right thing – she's still learning the ropes, making mistakes.

The other problem with detectives is that mostly they're not expected to make mistakes, and that's just so unlike real life. The problem we're by-passing is that crime fiction isn't like real life. There's a structure to it, and the structure is a puzzle. There's a crime, an investigation, then the revelation of who did it and that's not like real life. It doesn't work that way.

It's what people think of as falsely composed structure – critics often don't take the form seriously because they don't think that's how the world is. But literary fiction also imposes a structure on the world that isn't there. Countless literary novels are just over-literate people talking the way people *don't* really talk and reacting to situations in a way they wouldn't react in real life. So all fiction is a construct; it's just that literary fiction's been getting away with it for far too long.

Ian Rankin

The Naming of the Dead

A Fragment of a New Novel

Ian Rankin

In place of a closing hymn, there was music. The Who, 'Love Reign O'er Me'.

Rebus recognised it the moment it started, thunderclaps and teeming rain filling the chapel. He was in the front pew; Chrissie had insisted. He'd rather have been further back: his usual place at funerals. Chrissie's son and daughter sat next to her. The daughter, Lesley, was comforting her mother, an arm around her as the tears fell. The son, Kenny, stared straight ahead, storing up emotion for later. Earlier that morning, back at the house, Rebus had asked him his age. He would be thirty next month. Lesley was two years younger. Brother and sister looked like their mother, reminding Rebus that people had said the same about Michael and him: *the pair of you, the spit of your mum.* Michael … Mickey if you preferred. Rebus's younger brother, dead in a shiny-handled box at the age of fifty-four. The full post-mortem hadn't come through yet. Massive stroke was what Chrissie had told Rebus on the phone, assuring him that it was 'sudden' – as if that made a difference.

'Sudden' meant Rebus hadn't been able to say goodbye. It meant his last words to Michael had been a joke about his beloved Raith Rovers in a phone call three months back. A Raith scarf, navy and white, had been draped over the coffin alongside the wreaths. Kenny was wearing a tie that had been his dad's, Raith's shield on it – some kind of animal holding a belt-buckle. Rebus had asked the significance, but Kenny had just shrugged. Looking along the pew, Rebus saw the usher make a gesture. Everyone rose to their feet. Chrissie started walking up the aisle, flanked by her children. The usher looked to Rebus, but he stayed where he was. Sat down again so the others would know they didn't have to wait for him. The song was only a little over halfway through. It was the closing track on *Quadrophenia*. Michael had been the big Who fan, Rebus himself preferring the Stones. Had to admit though, albums like *Quadrophenia* and *Tommy* did things the Stones never could. Daltrey was whooping now that he could use a drink. Rebus had to agree, but there was the drive back to Edinburgh to consider. The function room of a local hotel had been booked. All were welcome, as the minister had reminded them from the pulpit. Whisky and tea would be poured, sandwiches served. There would be anecdotes and reminiscences, smiles, dabs at the eyes, hushed tones. The staff would move quietly, out of respect. Rebus was trying to form sentences in his head, words which would act as his apology.

I need to get back, Chrissie. Pressure of work.

He could lie and blame the G8. That morning in the house, Lesley had said he must be busy with the build-up. He could have told her, I'm the only cop they don't seem to need. Officers were being drafted in from all over. Fifteen hundred were coming from London alone. Yet Detective Inspector John Rebus seemed surplus to requirements. Someone had to man the ship – the very words DCI James Macrae had used, with his acolyte smirking by his shoulder. DI Derek Starr reckoned himself the heir apparent to Macrae's throne. One day, he'd be running Gayfield Square police station. John Rebus posed no threat whatsoever, not much more than a year away from retirement. Starr himself had said as much: *nobody'd blame you for coasting, John. It's what anyone your age would do.* Maybe so, but the Stones were older than Rebus; Daltrey and Townshend were older than him, too. Still playing, still touring. The song was ending now, and Rebus rose to his feet again. He was alone in the chapel. Took a final look at the purple velvet screen. Maybe the coffin was still behind it; maybe it had already been moved to another part of the crematorium. He thought back to adolescence, two brothers in their shared bedroom, playing 45s bought down Kirkcaldy High Street. 'My Generation' and 'Substitute', Mickey asking about Daltrey's stutter on the former, Rebus saying he'd read somewhere that it was to do with drugs. The only drug the brothers had indulged in was alcohol, mouthfuls stolen from the bottles in the pantry, a can of sickly stout broken open and shared after lights-out. Standing on Kirkcaldy promenade, staring out to sea, and Mickey singing the words to 'I Can See For Miles'. But could that really have happened? The record came out in '66 or '67, by which time Rebus was in the Army. Must have been on a trip back. Yes, Mickey with his shoulder-length hair, trying to copy Daltrey's look, and Rebus with his forces crop, inventing stories to make army life seem exciting, Northern Ireland still ahead of him …

They'd been close back then, Rebus always sending letters and postcards, his father proud of him, proud of both the boys.

The spit of your mum.

He stepped outside. The cigarette packet was already open in his hand. There were other smokers around him. They offered nods, shuffling their feet. The various wreaths and cards had been lined up next to the door, and were being studied by the mourners. The usual words would crop up: 'condolence' and 'loss' and 'sorrow'. The family would be 'in our thoughts'. Michael wouldn't be mentioned by name. Death brought its own set of protocols. The younger mourners were checking for text messages on their phones. Rebus dug his own out of his pocket and switched it on. Five missed calls, all from the same number. Rebus knew it from memory, pushed the buttons and raised the phone to his ear. Detective Sergeant Siobhan Clarke was quick to answer.

"I've been trying you all morning," she complained.

"I had it switched off."

"Where are you anyway?"

"Still in Kirkcaldy."

There was an intake of breath. "Hell, John, I completely forgot."

"Don't worry about it." He watched Kenny open the car door for Chrissie. Lesley was motioning to Rebus, letting him know they were headed for the hotel. The car was a BMW, Kenny doing all right for himself as a mechanical engineer. He wasn't married; had a girlfriend but she hadn't been able to make it to the funeral. Lesley was divorced, her own son and daughter off on holiday with their dad. Rebus nodded at her as she got into the back of the car.

"I take it you're phoning for a gloat?" Rebus started walking towards his Saab. Siobhan had been in Perthshire the past two days, accompanying Macrae on a recce of G8 security. Macrae was old pals with Tayside's Assistant Chief Constable. All Macrae wanted was a nosey, his friend happy to oblige. The G8 leaders would meet at Gleneagles Hotel, on the outskirts of Auchterarder, nothing around them but acres of wilderness and miles of ring-fenced security. There had been plenty of scare stories in the media. Reports of 3,000 Marines landing in Scotland to protect their president. Anarchist plots to block roads and bridges with hijacked trucks. Bob Geldof had demanded that a million demonstrators besiege Edinburgh. They would be housed, he said, in people's spare rooms, garages and gardens. Boats would be sent to France to pick up protesters. Groups with names like Ya Basta and the Black Bloc would aim for chaos, while the People's Golfing Association wanted to break the cordon to play a few holes of Gleneagles' renowned course.

"I'm spending two days with DCI Macrae," Siobhan was saying. "What's to gloat about?"

The Naming of the Dead will be published by Orion on 18 October, 2006

Belinda Cooke

From the Russian of Marina Tsvetaeva

Marina Tsvetaeva's muse is passion: for life, places and above all lovers and fellow poets. This only heightens the nature of her personal tragedy. With her husband and daughter imprisoned, and excluded from the poetic community in Russia and abroad, she had no practical means of supporting herself and her son. She said around this time, 'I don't want to die, I just want not to be.' Feeling she had no other exit, she was driven to suicide in Elabuga on 31 August 1941.

An Attempt at Jealousy

So what's it like
living with some other woman?
Simpler is it? With just one stroke of the oar
can the memory of me, an island
floating in the sky not on the water,

have so quickly faded like
a receding shoreline …?
Oh souls, souls.
We should be sisters—
never lovers.

What's it like living
with an ordinary woman,
one who lacks the divine,
since (like you) your queen
has come down from her throne?

What's it like?
How do you eat, get up,
get about? Being so
ordinary and banal
how do you cope, poor man?

I've had it up to here with all this!
I must get my own place'—.
What's it like living with
any old person
you my chosen one?

Is the food more edible?
Does it suit you better?
(You can't complain if it makes you sick).
What's it like living with a mere semblance –
you who have walked on Sinai?

What's it like living with
a stranger to these parts?
Tell me straight, do you love her?
Or does Zeus's shame
hang upon your brow?

What's it like?
Can you possibly be in good health?
How do you sing?
With all that festering guilt on your conscience
how do you cope, poor man?

What's it like living
with trash from the market?
Are you paying the price?
After Carrara marble
What's it like living with crumbling plaster?

(God was carved out of a block
and has been completely destroyed.)
What's it like living with some
run-of-the mill woman,
you who have known Lilith?

Have you had enough of the latest
from the market? Has the novelty worn off?
What's it like living with
some earthly woman
without six senses?

Now, in all honesty are you happy?
No. No? What's it like living in
your bottomless pit my love?
Is it worse or the same
as my life with someone else?

No Doubt We'll Meet in Hell

No doubt we'll meet in hell, my passionate sisters,
and we'll drink hell's resin,
we, who with each vein
sang praises to the Lord.

We, who did not bend in the night
over the cradle or the spinning wheel,
have been carried away by an unsteady boat
under cover of a great cloak.

Dressed up since early morning
in delicate Chinese silk
we struck up heavenly songs
at the robber's camp fire.

Shoddy needlewomen
(however they sew it all comes apart),
dancers and pipers,
mistresses to the whole world.

One minute scarcely covered in rags
the next our hair plaited with constellations,
both in jails and summer walkways
having strolled the heavens

in the starlit night
in the orchard in paradise ...
I am sure we'll meet, loved girls
dear sisters, in hell.

No One Has Taken Anything Away

No one has taken anything away.
I am delighted that we are apart.
I kiss you across the
one hundred miles that divide us.

I know our gift is unequal,
my voice for the first time is silent.
Young Derzhavin, what can
my ill-bred verses signify to you?

I bless you on your fearful journey:
fly young eagle.
You managed to look directly at the sun.
Was my youthful gaze too intense?

No one gazed after you
with a more tender or irrevocable look ...
I kiss you across the
one hundred years that divide us.

You Throw Back Your Head

You throw back your head
so proud and full of talk.
This February has brought me
a lively travelling companion.

Rattling our Ukrainian gold ...
and slowly exhaling smoke,
as solemn strangers
we walk about our native town.

I don't ask whose hands carefully touched
your eyelashes, my beautiful one,
or when, and how, and with
whom, and how many times

your lips were kissed. My hungry spirit
has subdued that dream.
I honour that part of you which is
a god-like ten-year old boy.

Let us linger by the river which washes
the coloured beads of the street lamps.
I shall lead you as far as the square
where young tsars have been seen.

Whistle out your childish pain
and squeeze your heart in the palm of your hand ...
My composed and violent
emancipated slave, goodbye.

Marina Tsvetaeva

Bish

Alan McMunnigall

Bish is up the shops, kicking a ball about wi Pogo. It's the first time I've seen him since his bird Lydia dropped her wean, and this makes me look at him a wee bit differently. Mind you he still looks like he always did. He's dressed the same as usual in his Man U top, Nike cap and a pair of flashy trainers. He's thirteen years auld but I swear you'd think he was no more than ten or something – fucking wee babyface.

Alright Bish! I shouts over to him.

Alright, he shouts back. What you up to?

Fuck all, I says.

He passes the ball to us and I indulge in some keepy-uppy before knocking it onto Pogo who crashes the thing against the launderette shutters with a clatter. It's night and maist of the shops round here are shut: aw except the takeaway place, the chippy and the pub across the carpark. I watch as Bish controls the ball and dribbles it round a big slab of concrete that's lying on the ground, then he chips it to Pogo who traps it and sends in a pishy cross that's too long for anybody to reach. The ball goes bouncing along the empty carpark with Pogo chasing after it.

Bish turns to us. See that cunt, he says, don't know why he fucking bothers, the fat bastard canny move or nothing. You can see his tits jiggling when he runs. Should fucking well gie it up.

He looks over to see where Pogo has got to, then wipes his nose, leaving a wee trail of snot on the back of his hand. Fucking freezing, he mumbles, rubbing his arm then bending down to pick up a stone. I'm cauld, he goes, really fucking cauld. He waits a minute then turns and cracks the stone off the steel shutters of the launderette. Then he searches about for something else to throw, finds a bit of a broken ginger bottle with the Irn Bru label still stuck to it. He nudges it with his trainer, lifts it up and smashes it against the shutters. He starts laughing. You see that? You see that? I broke it to fuck man.

So you did, I says.

Broke it to fuck.

So you did.

Up the shops aw the shutters are covered in writing: GOD BLESS LOYALIST ULSTER, FUCK THE QUEEN, FUCK THE POPE, IRA, UDA, UVF … aw that sort've thing. Plus tons of mentions for people and weird shit like: AFRO JULIE SUCKS COCKS, SLEEPING TABLET IS GAY, THE POLIS EAT SHITE WAE FORKS AND SPOONS. At night Bish is usually at the same spot, drinking or playing fitbaw, and right enough, this is where he used to knock about with wee Lydia. That was until recently. He'd go round the back of the shops with her, round where the bins are. After twenty minutes he'd come back, position hissel in front of aw the wee dicks who gave him respect. When he knew Lydia was out of earshot he'd say stuff like: Jist got my hole there lads, ah jist banged Lydia round the back.

Bish likes to watch who goes in and out of the chippy. Sometimes he waits outside the Haddows pleading wi auld cunts to buy his booze for him – cans of TL, the big plastic bottles of Strongbow. If the polis show up he vanishes for a bit. Then he's back. His name is everywhere. BISH + POGO, BISH AND LYDIA, LYDIA lvs BISH, BISH MANCHESTER UNITED FC, BISH CELTIC CASUALS, BISH SYTO, BISH YA BAS ...

One night I was up here with him. We were with this Asian guy from school called Ziad. It was a while ago. Bish had a can of spray paint he'd nicked from a shop in the town so he brought it out and gave the three of us mentions on the shutters of the bookies. Then underneath it, for no reason, he goes and draws a swastika. A big fucking red swastika. And Ziad goes mental at him. What the fuck you do that for? he shouts. You shouldny draw that. You racist or something?

Naw, no me ... I'm no fucking racist, says Bish.

You shouldny have done it! Ziad nabs the can of spray paint and scores out the swastika. You shouldny have fucking did that, you shouldny have ... fuck sake!

Bish took the huff and telt him to get to fuck. He never spoke to Ziad again. For the next few weeks he went round spraying swastikas on every wall in Sighthill. It was like he had a fucking mission to do as many as possible. They were all over the joint – at the side of the maisonettes, under the blocks of flats, on the graveyard wall, the gravestones, on the chapel, round the community centre. Everywhere you looked. Next to one of them he wrote: ZIAD IS A PAKI CUNT. I mean, he was always a bit of a bastard, somebody you couldny trust. Even at school ... one minute he'd be your best mate, the next he'd be fucking you over.

Pogo has disappeared round the back of the shops, probably to have a pish or something. He's taken the ball away with him. This is meant to be summer but it's chilly as fuck and I'm standing here, shivering in ma short sleeved Celtic jersey. The shops are spookily quiet, jist the odd person nipping into the chip shop but that's about it. I glance at the watch I got for my birthday, see it's five past ten.

You got any fags? Bish goes to us.

Naw, I says.

None?

Naw, I've no got any.

He looks like he doesny believe me. You sure? he goes.

Honest Bish, I says, I've nay fags on us. You can search us if you don't believe me. I've been gasping the whole fucking day.

He sniffs. I've no got any.

Ay well, he says, so you say.

I haven't … honest to fuck!

While we're waiting for Pogo to return I decide to ask him about his wean. The cunt's just become a daddy, so I should say something. At least fucking mention the fact. It's a good opportunity. We've been talking about him in school and naybody can imagine him shoving a pram or changing nappies, it's too bizarre to get your head round – Bish the daddy – I mean, fuck sake!

Heard wee Lydia had the wean, I goes to him.

Silence.

Ay, I heard she had it. How's she doing?

How's who doing?

Lydia, I says. I heard she had the baby and that. How's she doing? She okay?

He takes off his Nike cap, scratches his heid and screws up his face at me. What you fucking talking about? He looks right at us. How the fuck would I know how she is?

I was only asking, I says to him.

He puts his cap back on and jabs his finger into ma chest. See if I find out you've been talking about this to anycunt … I'll kill you. That clear? Is it? If I find oot from anybody that you've said anything about me … I swear to fuck I'll kill you!

While he speaks I gaze at the ground, feeling wee flecks of his spittle landing on my face, on my cheeks, my lips. I want to wipe them away but I don't. I know it's the sort of gesture he'd notice and go fucking mental about. He's mental enough without me making him any worse.

That fucking clear?

Ay, nay offence Bish.

Fucking noising me up.

I wisny.

Ay you fucking were.

Nay offence and that.

I can hear the music blaring out from the pub across the carpark. It's country and western, the kind my da listens to when he's pished and there's nothing on the telly.

You sure you've nay fags on you?

Naw Bish, I told you. I've no had any since last night.

Fucking useless.

I casually wipe my face, hoping he doesny spot me doing it. I mention to him that I canny afford to buy any fags. This is true, I'm no making it up. Lately I've had to resort to pinching the odd yin from my da and he's begun to notice this. The other night he came into my room and said it was funny how fags came in packs of seventeen and eighteen these days. But Bish doesny believe me when I tell him this. His head is bowed and the brim of his cap stops me seeing his eyes properly. He's moving around on the spot, twitching. I can hear his breathing. He sniffs and spits on the ground. Piss off, he says, afore I lose my temper. You've went and put me in a bad mood.

Listen, I wisny spreading it about you and wee Lydia. I only heard it from somebody else. That's how come I was asking you. I don't even know what your wean is called or nothing.

Who telt you? Must've been somebody telt you cause it wisny me.

Don't know, I just heard it and that.

From who?

I don't know Bish. Everybody knows ... everybody in school knows. It's no like ... I mean, fucking hell man, it's no like it's a big secret, even the teachers know. People are being cool about it. It says something, y'know, it says something, you being a da. Something to be proud of and that.

He's tense and wired up and I want to get away from him. It's time to split. I can see the rage in his eyes, the way he's gritting his teeth. I go to leave but instead of walking away I take a few steps, glance back at him and say: Must be weird but, that's all I'm saying here Bish. Must be bloody weird having a wean and only being thirteen. It'd fucking freak me out man, the pressure and that.

Naybody asked you did they, he growls at me.

Naw ... I know that Bish, don't get fucking narky man. I was only saying.

Naybody asked you for your opinion did they. I'd keep my mouth shut if I was you. Know what I mean! I'd keep it shut. Fucking noising me up ya prick.

His words sting me a wee bit cause there used to be a time when we were good pals. But I feel sorry for him as well. He looks so fucking depressed, and from what I've heard he's been getting hassle from Lydia's ma. His whole life is fucked up, and he's only thirteen, so you have to pity him. Listen, I says, it's no that bad. Lydia's a nice wee bird, so nay bother there. I've always liked Lydia, always thought she was alright. I mean, she's a wee shag, eh!

YOU GO FUCKING SHAG HER THEN!

There's no point saying anything else. The conversation is finished. I say cheerio and head into the chippy where it's nice and warm. I order a roll and fritter and get the woman behind the counter to lash on plenty of salt and vinegar. My stomach has been grumbling the whole day and I've devoured maist of the roll before I'm away from the fucking counter. While I'm in the chippy I use the payphone to dial a mate of mine called Steph. It's his ma that answers the phone. When Steph comes on I tell him I'm up the shops.

Know what? I say to him.

What? he goes, sounding bored on the other end of the line.

I ran into Bish up here. And I asked him about wee Lydia and the wean. Don't think he was too fucking pleased, he wouldny talk about it, got pissed off and everything. Think him and Lydia must have split up.

Have they?

Think so anyhow.

Before my money runs out I tell Steph I'll see him later.

Outside I canny see Bish and it looks like he's fucked off. But then just as I'm going round the side of the post office I hear his voice whispering my name. His back is against the wall, his cap pulled down so you can hardly see his eyes. His hands are stuck in his pockets. He steps out from the shadows, all hunched up and threatening. C'mere a minute you, he says, peering over my shoulder.

I walk up to him, see his eyes darting from side to side. I'm wondering if Pogo is behind me or something. When I get close he takes off his cap, drops it on the ground. Then his face is about three inches from mine and before I can say anything he's jerked back his head and nutted me right on the bridge of my fucking nose. I let out a groan and step backwards, tripping over something that's lying behind me, I take a tumble, landing on my back. For some reason I canny make it up on my feet. I'm struggling and I must be down for a good thirty seconds before Bish comes into my vision, panting under the strain of a sizable chunk of concrete he's managed to lift up from the ground. It's like an old thick paving slab or something and the fucking thing is so heavy he has to struggle, carrying it at waist height, shuffling instead of walking.

Naw Bish … I hear myself pleading. The big vein in his neck is bulging out, his eyes are demented. I lift my hands to protect my face, turning weakly onto my side – the strength has disappeared from my body, like it's all been drained away and I canny move. You keep your mouth shut, he gasps. Keep it shut about me and Lydia in the future. He stands over me, making one last effort to hoist it up over his head.

John Purser

Dialogues Concerning Natural Religion

Columba to God

I have tried to know suffering as the birds know it
to hunger with the starved buzzard
to bruise as a redwing stupefied by storms
to share the cackling fears of the red heathercock.
I am no dove.

My pride has fed on corpses
stabbing the eye of knowledge,
a raven pecking at meanings
wanting possession of dead things.

My pens are tugged from the wings of geese
hissing their innocence,
the skins of hollies stripped and boiled
and insects crushed for ink.
Five hundred calves have crumpled to their knees
to yield pelts for my library of books.

Oh my God forgive! Forgive me – count my ribs –
I too have yielded one for Eves I never touched,
– through my coarse cloak they leave
their imprint on the strand –
I would have truly starved
but my kind acolyte slipped milk into my meal.

My only purity in song, I gladly sing.
My one sorrow in dying
to leave others sorrowing.

Columba to King David

You must have written more.
Three fifties?
I myself have covered more vellum than you papyrus.
No poet of your stature writes without foresight.
You have seen Christ crowning innocence
the dove over Jordan, water turned into wine,
and that head on silver in its sauce of blood.

Those poems, where have they gone?
What stopped your prophecy,
Strangled the duty of a bard?

Where was Isaiah if not here and now
before and after – ever with the truth?
What clogged your bowels?
Kingship?

Power and lust and at the latter end – unable.
Yet the Lord will shepherd you,
great poet that you were.
His sheepflock sing your every surviving word
through matins, lauds and vespers,
decades, centuries, a *laus perennis*.

Your harp? Had you but known –
your little lyre, was it as sweet
as the *tiompan*?

I too have cast my voice
beyond our mortalities.
Has anybody heard?

God give me grace that I may sing
in the same congregation
as you and the Cherubim.

A City Herald

High above the city roosts its true ruler –
The weathercock.

After a giddy night they greets the dawn
in glittering plumage, addressing their minds
to kingly thoughts and matters philosophical.

Humanity is beneath them
and they see nothing above
that is not a part of their own kingdom.

But a top-floor tenement boy with cheap telescope
also closes his night's watch.

And now, stravaiging through the square
with cockerel crow –
he passes people by
but, in his mind's eye, sees
the starlight pulsing
far beyond the sun.

Amoretti XVII

Today is your birthday
and you returning home.
I pick mussels at a low ebb tide
now turning in the shape of the new moon.
My back is bent to the work,
my hands near numb.

Streams from choked culverts
rattle down the track,
tracing fresh ways among the seaweed rocks,
and the wind
batters the sea with mad patterns.

Straightening, I know again
your absence
as a hurt beneath my rib.

Tonight we shall taste and eat
and I shall feel
your long spine, curved beside me:
and above the cool rise
of your shoulders
the nape of your neck
warm under your autumn hair.

Amoretti XX

You wear only a rainbow hat of straw
in the tepid water up to your shoulders
warm brown in ripples of sun.

I see you after towelling
on the shadowed path
your rainbow hat, face shaded,
white shirt, shorts, long limbs,
a deer's dappled impression.

On horseback now,
your swatch of hair
switching with flex of flanks,
and the horse's tail - two swathes
of sunlit growth.

Shall you put on your hat before the rain
or in the long grass shake
your loosened mane?

Tartan Noir
Invented Certainties in Mean Wynds

Edmund O'Connor

When James Ellroy called Ian Rankin 'King of Tartan Noir' for a book blurb it was just a cool-sounding name. But Tartan Noir is a curious example of how elements of recent Scottish writing can be hammered together to make a 'movement', or a 'pack'. Tartan Noir is the most noticeable publishing trend of the last 15 years, with more joining its ranks, largely because if crime sells; crime with a tartan twist should sell better. But is this movement anything more than Publisher's new clothes, with some very odd bedfellows bundled in there to shift product? Or is there something genuinely dark and disturbing scuttling the streets?

If this is a pack or gang, there have to be entry requirements: the subject-matter must be crime-related; and the crime should be written about Scotland and/or from a Scottish author, the former being more important. Val McDermid rarely strays into Scotland from her northern England stomping grounds, but she gets in for being one of the most brilliant crime writers around: to exclude her would be daft. Otherwise the house is open: Rankin, Manda Scott, William McIlvanney, Denise Mina all easily fit under the umbrella. For space reasons, I concentrate on established figures and notable new talent. Apologies to anyone left out.

Some terms need defined. 'Golden Age' refers not only to a time when writers like Agatha Christie, Ngaio Marsh and Dorothy L Sayers were prominent in crime writing, but also to a mood that pervades their books. The format of the Golden Age novel is that a crime is committed in a relatively perfect social order: sleuth beetles in, solves mystery and order is restored to the happy little universe. There's also the ritual humiliation of the bumbling police, the near-obligatory isolated setting – but the plot is key. Christie, Sayers and co. inherited this notion of ultimate social perfection from Conan Doyle (whose unhappy Inspector Lestrade had Sherlock Holmes running rings around him). The title of Sayers' *The Unpleasantness at the Bellona Club* both sums up the movement, and does the critics' work for them. Satirised, sneered at or worshipped, depending on taste, the Golden Age is now regarded as a museum-piece movement, and only through heavy adaptation or disguise can a writer produce something which is not instantly dismissed as old-fashioned.

Various hands did in the Golden Age, but conspirators-in-chief were Messrs Hammett and Chandler, who saw the antics of Poirot, Marple, Wimsey *et al* as a hopelessly inaccurate portrayal of crime. But all they did was create another slightly less inaccurate mode: the solo gumshoe, distrustful of authority, hitched to Colt revolvers, bottles of whisky and breathy blondes with a talent for trouble. With these trappings, they mired the form down so that others saw these outer garments as the whole, and produced hackneyed versions of an already-imperfect form.

'Police procedural' grew out of the gumshoe format, in that dirt, darkness and grime were stuck to both forms, but in the 'Procedural', there was a little more trust of the authorities to get their man. Its format centres on the police's role in identifying the crime, the criminal, and then his capture. The purest example is Ed McBain's *87th Precinct* series, where a bunch of tough-talking male cops operate in a fictional city (New York?) catching crooks and dragging them to justice through dirty streets. This form has survived for over 50 years, and is as prone to bastardisation as any other, but is surprisingly adaptable, from cosy academic deaths in Colin Dexter to the hard-hitting social comment of Sjöwall and Wahlöös.

The field splits hopelessly into sub-genres, but one deserves explanation: the psychological thriller. Other attempts at the genre don't try to get inside the head of the killer and/or victim, this one explicitly intends to. It's often a more subtle and effective form, more immune from superfluous baggage. It is also more accessible to female readers who are turned off by the Boy's Own adventures elsewhere: the investigator needs to have subtlety, understanding and cunning to track down the perpetrator, instead of just a handy way with roughing up informants.

Where to begin? With the master himself, Ian Rankin.

Most of Rankin's Inspector Rebus stories are good, but *Black and Blue* deserves especial attention. In these 498 pages, Rankin makes the leap from talented cult Scottish writer into being one of the best writers around. Marcel Berlins comments that with this, "Ian Rankin joins the élite of British crime writing". It also puts him head and shoulders above his Edinburgh rival, Quintin Jardine, in awareness and resonance.

The plot? Tangled to say the least. Rebus is supposed to be investigating the death of an oil worker from Aberdeen who has a terminal connection with a set of Edinburgh metal railings, but as ever with Rebus, this is not the full story. He's also taken a close interest in the 'Johnny Bible' killings, a series of murders which ape the style of the infamous 'Bible John' – Scotland's most notorious serial killer, still uncaptured. His interest in the original Bible John spirals into obsessive behaviour. But while Rebus is on this case, others are busy getting on *his* case. He's being hounded by a TV crew for involvement in the alleged frame-up of one Lenny Spaven, and is also the subject of an internal investigation. And since the internal investigator knows that Rebus suspects him of being paid off by gangsters, it's unlikely the verdict on Rebus will be lenient.

This is just the tip of the iceberg. The reader gets inside the mind of Bible John – still hunting for 'the upstart' (as he calls 'Johnny Bible') – and also gets a whirlwind tour of Scotland, from Rebus's home patch of Edinburgh to Glasgow, Aberdeen, North Sea oil rigs and even out to

Shetland. And much more. In the hands of any other writer, readers would soon be so bogged down in detail that they'd give up! But Rankin has learned James Ellroy's secret: keep your mind on one storyline at a time, but if it's reached a natural pause, simply divert to another one.

A key question for anyone used to detective fiction, especially the police procedural Rebus inhabits, is: Why doesn't Rebus bring in Bible John, giving the reader creative closure? But this would be too easy an ending, both for Scotland and the Inspector: Scotland have one less bogeyman (which would never do) while Rebus would become effectively bullet-proof for the rest of his career – creative suicide, in other words. There's unfinished business. And Rebus has a penchant for leaving loose ends.

But there's typical Rankin playfulness too: Rebus finds a copy of Iain Banks's *Whit* amongst the dead oil worker's 'personal effects' (two tips of the hat to his fellow Fifer: one on purpose, one by accident). Rebus also plays the Rolling Stones' album *Black and Blue* during one of his all-night brooding sessions: "Black influences, blue influences; not great Stones, but maybe their mellowest album". But this novel, with murders, beatings, drink and drugs, is not in the least mellow. A 'Major Weir' pops up too as head of an oil company, although students of Scottish religious history will know the name through a different route – that of a 17th-century Christian fanatic, otherwise known as 'The Wizard of West Bow', who confessed to incest and devil worship before being strangled and burnt. Oil and religion – both streams running deep in the nation's veins.

It is easy to see echoes of Hogg and Stevenson in Rankin's work, and Rankin makes no secret of these influences, but there is another whose shadow Rankin existed in, at least early on. William McIlvanney's novels *Docherty* and *Remedy is None* are critically-acclaimed masterpieces, but his Glasgow crime trilogy set the scene for what was to come, especially the first instalment, *Laidlaw*. In 280 pages, McIlvanney sets out one of the most idiosyncratic detectives of modern times: melding the hard boiled, tough-talking loner detective of the American tradition (Sam Spade etc.) with the humanist European, like Georges Simenon's Inspector Maigret.

Inspector Jack Laidlaw of Glasgow police is rudely grabbed from a disintegrating marriage by a murder in a park: that of a young girl, who has also been sexually assaulted. McIlvanney never alludes to it, but with the book being published in 1978, the Bible John murders were fresh in mind: he plays on folk memory with his choice of victim and location. Laidlaw's sidekick is Brian Harkness, a greenish rookie whose strident judgments are unsmoothed by experience while the Inspector, however, is all soft undulations in his thoughts, recognising shades of grey in life, death and crime and tries to explain them to the brash young officer:

"'What's murder but a willed absolute, an invented certainty? An existential failure of nerve. Faced with the enormity, they [people] lose their nerve, and where they should see a man, they see a monster.'"

William McIlvanney

Elsewhere he comments: "'Monstrosity's made by false gentility. You don't get one without the other. No fairies, no monsters. Just people. You know what the horror of this kind of crime is? It's the tax we pay for the unreality we choose to live in. It's a fear of ourselves.'"

The case takes a back seat to the observations and clashes in thought arising from it – the young pup expressing revulsion and contempt for the criminal; the old dog trying to explain the world doesn't come in two varieties of good and evil. One reason *The Papers of Tony Veitch* and *Strange Loyalties* don't work so well is that Laidlaw and Harkness have learned to work together – giving less scope for Laidlaw's existential witticisms.

Another thread is that of police and criminal uniting against a common enemy – the murderer. The police want to collar him as a murderer, the gangsters because honour's been invoked, and an unwanted murder's bad for business. The book becomes a race between the two sides to net the murderer first. Curiously, the murderer himself is relatively inactive: at the start, he's already committed the crime, and he spends the rest of the book in a hideout. But the book isn't really about him, but about the society that shaped him and its attitudes towards those beyond the pale.

The successful TV series *Taggart* should undoubtedly be seen as a major influence not only on Scottish crime writing in the 1980s, but ever since. Glenn Chandler, its creator and writer of many of its major stories, is an under-sung talent of Scottish crime writing, although he would probably resist being included in the Tartan Noir genre. His polished writing, stealing elements from *Dragnet* amongst others, created DI Jim Taggart of Maryhill CID (inspiringly played by Mark McManus). Mock if you like its formulaic plots (and plenty do: "There's been a murder" in a thick Glaswegian accent is a standard put-down) and in its early days, wobbly sets. But it has inspired writers to feel that Scottish crime stories are not only possible, but can find a ready audience. Though there are clear echoes of Laidlaw, *Taggart* has created an influence all its own, not to be dismissed by those who keep their noses in books.

One of most welcome aspects of Tartan Noir is the increased presence of women writers and a solid tackling of hard-edged topics, from bog-standard murder, to sexual and psychological abuse. The striking thing about many female Tartan Noir writers is their desire to get away from the staleness and occasional latent sexism McIlvanney and others are guilty of. They reject many of their predecessors' standards (though narratives can be twisted to serve their turn). Such is the weariness with the old detective/PI formulas, some, like Denise Mina or Manda Scott, use non-professional investigators who have a personal connection with the case, neatly upping the drama at a stroke. This has breathed new life into a genre sorely needing a pick-me-up, making it into one of the most exciting and stimulating areas of Scottish writing today.

Perhaps the most interesting of these authors is Val McDermid, a grand-master in two sub-genres of crime fiction. In the Kate Brannigan series, she creates an energetic, no-nonsense private eye whose take on the traditional macho gumshoe is a refreshing change. McDermid combines lightness of touch with a pacey and engaging plot. In the Tony Hill & Carol Jordan series, she moves into another gear with a nerve-shreddingly intense look inside the minds of serial killers, combined smoothly with a whiff of police procedural. In *Dead Beat*, our hero, of Brannigan and Mortensen Private Investigators, is engaged by a pop star, Jett to find Moira, his ex- songwriting partner/ old flame, who did a bunk just after he got big. Brannigan trawls the mean streets of Bradford, and turns up with Moira in tow. Moira knows she's stepping into a hornet's nest, but has little idea the sting will be lethal. Sure enough, she is found dead in the recording studio, her head smashed in with a saxophone.

Despite all the postmodern flourishes – Moira acquires a girlfriend as well as a heroin habit while AWOL, and the plot hinges on the wonders of modern technology – this is at heart a traditional Golden Age murder-at-the-manor for modern times. Like any good Poirot or Miss Marple tale, everyone in the house has a motive – from Jett's shady manager disliking

Val McDermid

Moira making waves in his dealings with Jett, to Jett's girlfriend who sees a rival for her meal-ticket. Add in a bumbling police inspector, a red herring, the theatrical final gathering of suspects in a single room ~ and picking the least likely suspect as the ultimate villain, you can't help feeling that McDermid is neatly paying her dues to the greats as well as finding a successful plot formula. Dame Agatha would have approved.

Brannigan is McDermid's answer to Sara Peretsky's V I Warshawski, a no-bullshit female PI from Chicago – Sam Spade with mascara. But Brannigan is more down to earth, more aware of her pitfalls – from trading banter with the company secretary to facing down cold-blooded murderers intent on getting away with their conservatory and remortgaging scams. She's tough, but knows when all she needs is a long bath and a Chinese take-away. An highly likeable character, Brannigan is the sort of PI you can imagine existing in the here-and-now, a rare thing these days. It helps that her base is Manchester and its environs, a world away from the mean streets of New York or the cool corruption of LA.

In books like *Wire in the Blood* she shows herself to be much more than a writer of pacey yarns. In the Tony Hill & Carol Jordan series, Hill is an ace psychological profiler, distrusted by run-of-the-mill cops who prefer traditional plod-work to headgames. Jordan, a senior policewoman, is his most trusted confidante, a keen champion of his methods – and would-be lover. But this soap dynamic is easily thrust into the background when they are tracking down the twisted serial killers. *Wire in the Blood* starts off in the mind of the killer, a TV celebrity, so no guessing-games there: the interest lies in how the coppers eventually catch up with him. Jacko Vance – one half of a Richard-and-Judy-style interviewing team – is a national treasure, which makes his being a serial killer all the more fantastic for the National Profiling Task Force, an élite unit created to deal with the outpouring of disturbed minds.

But serial killer he is, preying on young girls he meets at public events, seducing them, crushing their right arms in his Northumberland lair then throwing their chopped-up remains into a hospital incinerator. His public face and private horror are played off against each other. The 'normal' police are reluctant to believe Hill and Jordan, dismissing their theories as career-ending poppycock. So Hill, Jordan and the rest of the squad do it outside the official procedures after being warned off. They eventually catch up with him, but not before a few bodies have fallen.

Her crime fiction gives voice to marginalised sorts – worn-down barmaids, old soaks, low-level scamsters and others not usually associated with the genre: mainly lesbians and trans-sexuals. Brannigan is friends with a female couple, a key minor character in *Wire in the Blood* is lesbian, and Lindsey Gordon, whose series deserves more attention, is a lesbian journalist. But this subject, if handled at all in 'mainstream' crime fiction, often appears like a prurient soft-porn dream. In McDermid's hands it is treated as it should: neither glossed over nor leered at, just something

Denise Mina (© Colin McPherson)

someone is. McDermid's genius here is to mix police procedural with psychological terror: just when we are getting in too deep, the reader is pulled back into a (relatively) reassuring world of order and discipline.

Denise Mina is also adept at the psychological thriller, except there are no police at the centre. In *Garnethill*, Mina's debut, the murderer of Maureen O'Donnell's boyfriend is found by Maureen herself. A former victim of sexual abuse, she tracks down the killer through her own insights. The police again are at best unhelpful and in fact directly hinder her, suspecting her to be the killer with her history of mental problems. When she catches up with the killer, in Millport on Arran, she devises a fitting punishment: tricking him into swallowing an overdose of hallucinogenic drugs, making him as helpless as the women he preyed on.

The striking aspect of *Garnethill* and its follow-ups is not that the killer is finally unmasked, but we are led to sympathise almost automatically with Maureen, whose determination to find the killer outweighs any fragility and victimhood status she might have. Mina shows that victims, especially female ones, are actually able to act against their wrongdoers in ways the police could never imagine, let alone allow. The crime is not some abstract problem to be solved on the chalk board, but a living, breathing thing that needs all the investigator's experience to tackle.

Manda Scott also has an investigator with a personal stake in the case: in *Hen's Teeth* Kellen Stewart's ex-girlfriend is found murdered, stuffed full of Temazepam, which leads her down a route of pharmaceutical and genetic intrigue. Again, the police are clueless, as well as actively hostile towards Kellen, leaving her as the only one who can solve the murder. The novel is told from a first-person perspective: the reader identifying with her in a way unexpected for a crime thriller. In a vicarious manner, the reader *becomes* the investigator, an active participant instead of just a passive observer. The tension is not just the character's, it becomes the reader's property too, making it a much more intimate and fiery read.

Night Mares, sequel to *Hen's Teeth*, follows in much the same vein. The reader is taken on an impressionistic and emotional journey unlike any other, with horses dropping dead in a Glasgow vet school from a virulent strain of E Coli, resistant to all sterilisation measures. Unsurprisingly, the morale of the place takes a beating, especially Kellen's patient Dr Nina Crawford, whose mental health is at best precarious. Gradually it turns from simple bad luck to a vendetta, with Crawford's home being burnt down. As Crawford's friend and therapist, Stewart can't help get involved, as anyone who thinks the following would: "All I know is that the shade of her eyes changes as she walks closer to the depths of her own private hell and that the darker they are, the worse it is." With Scott combining emotional vividness and sure-footed specialist knowledge, *Night Mares* sucks the reader in to the point of claustrophobia.

So does Tartan Noir exist? Certainly, something does. The fact that

Manda Scott

writers like McDermid, Rankin and Guthrie have been bundled into one package is a triumph of publishers' spin-machines – each has her own ideas about how crime is tackled. But there does seem to be a trend, increasingly with female writers – a crucial reply to generations of male crime writers who may have had the arrogance to feel the genre theirs by right. McDermid, Scott and Mina have created a viable place for female crime writers in Scotland, with others like Alex Gray and Lin Anderson reaping the benefits. Marginalised voices, which women have always been, are now being heard. Personal experience rather than objective description informs female writers: McDermid with the media, Scott in the veterinary surgery and Mina with her forays into mental illness and female offenders. While traditional voices like Jardine, and semi-traditional ones like Rankin and McIlvanney will always have a hold on the reader's imagination, the most interesting road to the future lies with female writers, so long ignored or treated as special cases in crime fiction.

There will always be the camp-followers, authors who ride on a genre's coat-tails because of fashion, and Tartan Noir is no exception. Advocates of Tartan Noir should not be satisfied to see crime fiction considered an *equal* genre to literary fiction, but a *superior* one. Literary fiction has now detached itself into its own hermetic bubble away from the rest of the world, where people do and say things that are excused from reality because they are 'literary'. Despite its faults (and it has many) crime fiction is more relevant to us and our situation because, from leaders declaring war for ropey reasons, to smokers daring to puff in an enclosed public space, everyone has broken the law. We are all criminals.

Peter Snow

Lap Dog

To John Bellany

No whining tail-thumper, you,
no eager, barking, soulful-eyed best friend.
Who would throw a stick for you,
or rubber ball, sticky with your spit?

Your breath would rust gold rings,
rot the flesh slowly from the bones.
You haunt the desolation
from the dream-rooms to the quays,

and where the dead-eyed fishes
shine in cold embraces.
It was you, wasn't it,
who snuffed and slithered

under the gate of the artist's ribs,
winding yourself into his guts,
gnawing into his liver
to make your thirst his.

But creation triumphed over pain,
and he made a lap dog of you after all.
Now sunlight streams in the dream rooms;
carnivals and open-air cafes

are luminous in all their colours.
The artist is alive,
and you are his creature.

Some Corner of a Field

What fits the hand so snugly,
so convincingly, as a gun?
The gun exalts you.

You become a messenger,
a minor angel, of a sort.
And it was, I insist, necessary.

The soil was barren, sour;
nothing would grow in these scorched furrows.
Excited by the devastation,

I tore her clothes, beat,
scratched, bit, kicked.
She fought, but her flesh

leaped out to receive me:
and at last, penetration.
She was wet in spite of herself,

wet in self-defence.
Her nails dug long
lace-edged trenches in my back.

Afterwards I noticed the trees
were all sooty splinters;
even the crows had left

for the battlefields, probably.
And so my index finger bent
round the trigger, the beckoning gesture,

and so was sown the salt of my passion
to enrich the soil of this sad land,
that I love intensely as an angel.

Birthday Letter Unsent

Because he had hurt you
I seized him by the root of the tongue,
my tongue, and heaved him out

on to the grass, the pale creature.
He lay gasping, boneless and pathetic,
slippery with mucus, frog-eyes rolling.

Because he had hurt you,
I cut his throat,
and bled him into a bucket

and burned him all to ashes.
But the wind blew the ashes
into the bucket,

and they turned into hoodie crows
that pecked the eyes of motherless lambs
and climbed into the air on ragged wings.

I tried to catch them, but they flew away.
Now they squat upon your rooftop,
shrieking hoarsely at your hoodie-crows on mine.

Out-Patient

His body hung on him as awkwardly
as his institutional clothes,
his eyes glazed like pots,

scabs of bad falls crusting his cheeks and brow.
He stared through the periscope of his soul
at God-knew-what petrifying Gorgon

or Sphinx, with its insistent riddle.
He held out a hand flapping
like the wing of a wounded bird.

I bought him off with some guilty silver,
and he pushed himself off, tied together
with the chafing strings

of our judgments and charity,
unable to solve any riddle,
already turning to stone.

Mary

A bright autumn day
                with high clouds scudding
and the smell of bonfires;
                red and golden leaves
dancing in wind coils in the gardens.

A winter night
                and the stars are brilliant.
The Northern Lights throb and flicker
                over the luminous snow-fields.

A spring day with sunlight
                moving in the trees.
Swans are gliding on the river:
a flock of doves descends in unison
on the red roof-tiles.

A summer evening thick with stars,
                and a ceilidh in the light
of coloured bulbs; the scent
                of pine from the hills;

something calling from the wood
                to the lovers at the open gate.

Charles Got Lost in the Shuffle

Ted Fink

Charles was arrested on what is known in the 'hood' as a humbug.

A humbug: an outrageous, trumped-up, bogus arrest.

You might say I inherited Charles. He lived in an apartment building I purchased several years back. I would guess he's in his middle forties, short, balding and black. He keeps his place clean, pays his rent on time and does odd jobs to earn his way. I pay him a small monthly fee to sweep the sidewalks and clean the halls. It's true that he sometimes talks and laughs to himself, but I have personally never had a problem with Charles. And yes, he does play drums. Not real drums – fanciful ones. Sometimes, he says, when he is feeling good, he can hear the music and must keep time with that imaginary drum kit and those imaginary sticks.

On 28 January 1999 the police were hunting a man who, two weeks before, allegedly chased a thirteen-year-old girl down the street and yelled that he was going to get her. Charles was sweeping the sidewalk when a police car pulled up in a hurry and two officers hopped out. Sweeping the sidewalk must have seemed extremely suspicious. Why, would someone be sweeping the sidewalk on a street where no one ever swept the sidewalk? His response was a befuddled shrug of the shoulders, which demanded more questions. Name. Address. Basic information. Within minutes they left and Charles went back to his sweeping.

Approximately four months later the police came back in force. They arrested Charles as soon as he answered the door and threw him in jail. He was charged with three misdemeanours: making terrorist threats, corrupting the morals of a minor, and stalking. Charles remained in jail for eight days until his sister found out where he was and bailed him out with $150. On release he was told it had all been a mistake, a case of mistaken identity, because the initial report said they were looking for a man who was tall and of a light complexion. Charles was short and dark. But to clear matters up, he had to appear in court the following week to have papers signed and facilitate the return of his bail.

Unfortunately, at this hearing, Charles seemed a bit disturbed, a tad irritated and somewhat uncooperative. The judge took note of this and asked, "Sir, are you angry?" And when Charles muttered 'Yes', his Honourable ordered psychological tests. The following week the examining psychiatrist also found him to be not only upset and uncooperative but, in his opinion, paranoid. The psychiatrist, Dr. Stanton Roberts then declared Charles incompetent.

Nearly two years later I saw Charles and realised I hadn't seen him playing the drums for some time and that he seemed depressed.

"Hey, my man, no drums today?"

"No. I stopped playing."

"Yeah, how come?"

"I'm just not hearing the music any more."

"I'm sorry to hear that." I had just been making idle conversation, but it became clear that Charles had been waiting for me.

"Can you help me?" There was a look of desperation on his face. "Would you read these documents," he asked in his clipped way of talking, "and tell me what these people want?" He then handed me a stack of papers. "What do they want from me?"

There must have been twenty-five documents dating back to June of 1999. Each set of papers represented a different scheduled hearing; each had the card of a different public defender. The most important document, the one on top, was the bench warrant for his arrest. His crime: failing to appear. "Did you appear?" I asked.

"I did!" he said emphatically. "I was there. This has been going on for eighteen months. I need help, please!"

"I'll make some calls," I told him reluctantly.

Every month, for nearly two years Charles had received notices telling him to report to court to stand before the judge to have the matter resolved. The Public Defenders Office was representing him, but he didn't have one particular attorney. Charles became the client of the public defender assigned to the court that day. He began to get lost in the shuffle. Every month, even though he showed up and waited till the place closed, nothing was ever done, no public defender talked to him about the case. On 11/6/00, he didn't respond when they called his name – a bench warrant was immediately ordered for his arrest. Charles had gone to the bathroom just before his name was called.

It took me two hours of calling David Rose, the supervisor at the public defender's office. Rose urged me to bring Charles in and have him surrender himself voluntarily, because: "Ignoring a bench warrant," he said, "was *far more serious* than chasing a young girl down the street. This could *really* get a person arrested. If the police pick him up before he comes in on his own he could get up to two years. If he surrenders himself we should have no trouble getting the charges dismissed. Charles had never been arrested before or since," Rose reasoned. "The DA probably won't even be able to get the '*chased girl*' to show up."

But Rose confessed: Charles was caught in a legal catch 22.

The dilemma was this: For Charles to stand before the judge he had to be competent. And in order for him to achieve competence, according to the psychiatrist, he needed to go to a clinic and be medicated. But Charles didn't want to be treated with drugs so he immediately fell into a state of limbo and an endless vicious circle. He became part of a judicial shuffle-dance, shuffling back and forth between the psychiatrist's office and the court. A shuffle-dance of this ilk is the worst kind of municipal hoedown.

The next day when I bought Charles in I told Rose how Charles felt about the clinic and being medicated. Rose was sympathetic. A person shouldn't be forced to take drugs. But, if he didn't at least try to get competent so that he could stand before the judge he would soon miss one of his monthly trips to court and a new bench warrant would be issued for his arrest. The thing would start all over again. I was aghast! What a waste of time, money and energy! I am not, God knows, a Good Samaritan. But I had resigned myself to seeing this boondoggle through. But, most of all, I didn't want to do it again in six months. Rose saw I was worried and shook his head sadly, "Charles is just not competent."

"Are you sure? How do you know? He seems competent to me."

"Here. I'll show you. Charles," he said. "Do you know what I do?"

Charles smiled, raising one eyebrow. "No, I don't know what you do."

"Do you know why you're here?"

"No, I do not!"

"Do you know what you've been charged with?"

"I know that whatever it is, I am innocent."

"What does a judge do?"

Charles thought seriously. "I don't know exactly."

"What does the prosecutor do?

"I don't know."

"See!" Rose said declaring him incompetent. Charles, he insisted, had to go to the clinic and be medicated so that he could become competent.

"Rose, how are drugs going to make him know what you do or what a judge does? Are drugs going to make him smart? If drugs could make people smart we'd be giving kids drugs all day long. Serving them up at recess with soft pretzels and milk. Charles is not incompetent; he's stupid! I believe Charles is competent. I want to get this thing resolved."

"Charles," I said as we walked out of the courthouse, "you have a choice. If you don't want to go to the centre for therapy you can walk away and be arrested at some later date or … you can play the game. Go before the psychiatrist and answer the questions he asks you. If you want I'll give you the answers, I'll tell you what to say. The only way you can get rid of this charge and get your bail money back is to stand before the judge. And the only way that can happen is if you play the game."

"I never wanted to be in this game. I never asked to play."

The new evaluation was scheduled for18 December. Rose's quiz had given me some idea as to the questions the psychiatrist might ask and Charles supplied the rest. Dr Roberts had asked the exact same questions in each of his five previous meetings.He had asked Charles if he knew the role of the judge and prosecutor. And Charles answered him honestly that he wasn't sure. Then as Charles put it, "He asked some riddles"

"Riddles? Like what?"

"The first was, 'Why does a stitch in time save nine?'"

"What did you say?"

"I said, 'That if you fix something when it first breaks it'll save you a lot of fixin later on'."

"Good. What else?"

"He asked 'Why is a penny saved like a penny earned?' And I said, 'if you saved money it was like you worked for it cause you had it when you needed it'."

"That's acceptable. Go on."

"Then he asked me – and I'm still trying to figure out how he knew 'cause it happened way back in Junior High. He asked what happened when me and my best friend got caught smoking behind the school? At first I had to think back 'cause we weren't really caught 'cause we saw the principal coming and ditched the smokes."

"Is that what you told Dr. Roberts?"

"Well, yeah. I was kind of amazed that he knew about that. It made me laugh right out loud." Charles smiled but added that the doctor didn't think it was very funny.

Roberts was surprised when he saw me with Charles. He raised a sarcastic eyebrow when I told him I was acting as advocate for Charles. He ushered us into the dishevelled room that barely held the two chairs in front of his desk. Roberts was a well-groomed man in his early sixties. His hair was white, his complexion ruddy; dressed in his dark suit and tie. When he sat down he seemed to be right on top of us. So close you could smell his after-shave. Roberts leaned even closer and studied Charles.

"How are you feeling, Charles?" he asked.

"Fine. Fine." Charles answered.

He nodded and began by asking the meaning of the two sayings, how does a stitch in time save nine? And, why is a penny saved like a penny earned? Charles answered both of the questions correctly.

"When was the last time I saw you?" He asked, studying Charles' file.

"October the 12th, this year."

"That's right. Do you feel there have been any changes since then?"

"Yes sir."

"Have you gone for treatment? To be medicated?"

"I went to the clinic but I didn't get medicated."

At this point I stepped in. "Charles doesn't want to take drugs. Charles now understands fully what he has to do to be rid of these false charges. We talked to Rose and he feels that Charles is ready to stand before a judge and that the case will be dismissed. He has never been in trouble before or since and he *is* innocent of the charges."

Stanton nodded to me as if to say, 'uh-huh' and turned back to Charles. He swivelled in his chair and thumbed through the open folder on his desk. "If you did stand before a judge, how would you plead?"

Charles shrugged, "Not guilty."

"What does a judge do?"

"He decides whether I'm guilty or not."

"What does a public defender do?"

"He defends me."

"A district attorney?"

"He prosecutes me."

"What would happen if you pled 'guilty'?"

"I would go to jail."

"If the judge found you 'not guilty' what would that mean to you?"

Charles shrugged, "That I'd be free to go."

"That's right. Free to go. Do you know what you're charged with?"

"Making terrorist threats, and chasing some young girls down the street, but that's not true. It's just a charge."

"What do you think of Mr Rose?"

Charles couldn't for the moment think who Mr Rose was.

"Do you know who Mr Rose is?"

Charles looked over to me. But Stanton told him not to. "He's your public defender ..."

I said to Charles, "The supervisor we met the day I took you in."

"What do you think of Mr Rose?" Roberts demanded.

"I don't know what to think?"

"But he's your attorney? Do you trust him?"

Charles looked over to me. "I trust him," he said, pointing to me.

"Charles gets a new public defender assigned to him every time he goes to court. He's had eighteen different attorneys."

"Of course." Roberts said smugly. Then he launched into a series of questions to which if Charles answered 'yes' it would prove conclusively that he needed treatment.

"Charles do you see little green men?"

"No."

"Are secret agents following you around?"

"No."

"Do you see polka dot people?"

"No I do not."

"Are you influenced by outside forces?

"Yes I am," Charles answered. My heart sank.

A huge 'I gotcha' grin appeared on Roberts' face. "And what are those forces?" Roberts' eyes were full of delight.

"Intelligent people."

"And where do you meet these *intelligent* people?"– almost in a laugh.

"Well I don't actually meet them. I see them and hear them?"

Roberts could barely contain his glee. "And where do you see them and hear them?"

"On radio and TV!"

The smile disappeared from the Doctor's face. "Really? And what do they influence you to do? What things do they encourage you to do?"

Charles thought. "Well, like buy things…"

"Buy things?"

"Yeah, like commercials influence me to buy things and such."

"They do?"

"Yeah. Yes."

· Doctor Roberts looked at me. "Well, he needs some help there." It was an attempt at a joke, but no one was laughing. "Charles, are you angry?"

"No. Not now."

"Do you feel as if you're being persecuted?"

"Yes."

"How's that?"

"Being here. This is a form of persecution."

It was obvious from Dr. Roberts' frown that he didn't like that answer. I jumped into the fray. "Doctor, he was thrown in jail for seven days for something he didn't do. He has every right to feel persecuted."

"Yes, but that happened over a year ago. There's no reason to…"

"And he's still here! Still trying to get this thing resolved."

Roberts reluctantly agreed that Charles was competent and able to stand before the judge. The whole visit took six minutes.

The waiting room for courtroom B is the size of a football field. By ten past nine this capacious chamber is almost full. People are standing in line just to sign in. The court clerk sitting behind the desk is a big man, the size of a linebacker, who will obviously tolerate no nonsense. There are about 250 people in this room and there is no nonsense. Charles gets in line and signs in. We sit and wait. He reads his paper and I read mine.

By 9:30 I have finished the news and start on the crossword puzzle. So far nothing of significance has happened. By 10.00 I have completed the puzzle and have started the cryptogram. People, attorneys and court officials, go in and out but no one seems to have a sense of what is happening. The court is like a sealed vault. No Public Defender has come out to speak to Charles, to ask for Charles, to brief Charles. I begin to get edgy and go to the big court clerk sitting behind the desk. He only tells me to sit down. I begin to pace. In my naiveté I thought this would be the end of it. But by 10:30 I am getting a queasy feeling. My folly is in over-estimating the bureaucracy. The week before I had made many calls in an attempt to speak to a Public Defender, any Public Defender, but kept getting machines. I left messages but no one returned my calls. OK, but surely they would talk to us on court day. Frustrated, I begin to ask people emerging from the courtroom, dressed in suits, if they are with the Public Defenders office. No one is. I ask the court clerk, "Is there a Public Defender in there?" I get no answer, just a cold aggravated stare.

Occasionally someone emerges from the court and shouts a name.

Twice someone in handcuffs is brought through the waiting room and ushered into the court.

At 11:00 Charles is relaxed, still reading his paper, but I am starting to get upset. What the hell am I doing here? I have a business to run. Time is of the essence. Sitting behind me a husband and wife find my agitation humorous and smile, knowingly. "Is this your first time?" They ask. They tell me to relax. This is their 37th time! At 11:30 other people are starting to get disturbed. I am not alone in my pacing, trying to get a glimpse inside the court, and checking my watch. Those of us who are new are asking each other what the hell is going on? But Charles and the others, who have been there before are seated calmly, waiting.

At 11:45 there is an audible sigh of relief. The big court clerk emerges from the court with a bunch of papers that he waves over his head. Without his having said a word people start to form a line in front of his desk. He calls their names and gives them each a document. Suddenly, I realise that, for me, this is bureaucratic purgatory. Forget going to jail. The waiting in line to find out whether or not I was going to go to jail would be enough to drive me crazy! It's a wonder more people don't go bonkers and suffer from *court rage!* To my surprise, the court clerk calls Charles' name. We go up to the desk. "What's this paper?" I ask.

"His case has been pushed back. He's to reappear next month."

"What?!" I shout. I am actually jumping up and down. "This man has been here 18 times! This man was thrown in jail for a crime he didn't commit. This is total crap! What the hell is going on?"

I am livid. Charles is trying to calm me down!

"You got a problem, talk to his attorney."

"His attorney is the public defender."

"Well, she's inside."

I start to walk toward the courtroom, but the big guy tells me not to open the doors. "You open that door and I'll have you arrested!"

In my life I have taken many chances. I've climbed mountains, faced killer storms at sea, scuba-dived for buried treasure, but for the first time in my life I am frightened. I'm frightened of being charged, like Charles, with a misdemeanour! Because, in the city of Philadelphia, if you are charged with a misdemeanour, which I am sure opening the courtroom doors would be construed as, you get thrown in jail and become part of a criminal 'reserve' unit destined to be present at a once-a-month meeting in the purgatory known as the Philadelphia Court System.

Charles urges me to be cool. But I am fuming. Later that day, Rose who tells me the public defender that day had thirty-seven cases to deal with. "The case was postponed because the girl accusing Charles didn't show up. And if the girl doesn't show up next time, it'll be postponed again."

I was beside myself. "Isn't this a misdemeanour?" A parking ticket is a misdemeanour! He's already spent eight days in jail. He's been back to court 18 times! It's a misdemeanour, for crying out loud!"

"Yes, but in the city of Philadelphia a misdemeanour is punishable by up to five years in jail and this misdemeanour has got to be resolved in court, by the judge. But, you are right, it is a misdemeanour and, even if he's found guilty he won't serve time."

My heart sank. I felt the public defender's office was willing to let Charles be found guilty and would not be upset if he was. "Enough is enough! This case should be thrown out now!" was all I could say.

But it wasn't thrown out. It went on and on. And, it didn't matter that Charles had never been in trouble before or since or that he had been jailed for eight days, the waiting continued into the following month.

On the day Charles finally stood before the judge, Sarah Hawes was the Public Defender. Hawes had been assigned forty-four cases that day and it was only her third week on the job. She did come out to meet with Charles, but was hot under the collar because of the load and didn't want to talk to me about the case, citing confidentiality. Charles was sitting right next to me. I told her I could fill her in on the details of the case, which I knew better than she did. Reluctantly, she let me. It went in one ear and out the other. She had little time to talk, and less to listen, let alone remember. The fact that Charles spent a week in jail didn't mean a thing. The fact that he was arrested four months after the alleged offence occurred was not noted. That he had no record seemed irrelevant. "We'll plead innocent to all charges." She said flatly, checking her watch. "She knows what she's doin'," Charles said after she left …

The halls of justice appeared uncharacteristically well oiled that day. Still it was well after 2 pm when Charles was called before the bench. He was told to stand next to his PD and not to say anything. I was allowed to be present but only if I remained silent.

The girl who had been chased was now fourteen and seemed very shy. Her head was down, her eyes glued to the floor. She seemed more frightened of her mother, who had angrily taken off from work to accompany her, than anyone else. "I was on my way to school. He chased behind me. Not far. Just a few steps. He said he was gonna get me. He only said it once. I only saw him that one time." This terse testimony was enough for the district attorney to demand indignantly that the charges of stalking, corrupting the morals of a minor, and making terrorist threats all be considered in the first degree.

Judge Bruno said he would consider that recommendation and told the public defender to begin her cross-examination.

Sarah Hawes was sensitive to the girl, but failed to find out exactly what happened. She forgot that originally the police were looking for a tall light skinned African American. It had been two years since the alleged incident took place. Charles had changed. But Sarah Hawes did not ask the girl to look at Charles. She could have said, *Look at this man.*

Are you absolutely sure this is the man? Why do you think he chased you? Did you say anything to Charles that might have precipitated his behaviour? Were you and your friends making fun of him? Were you joking with your friends when it happened? What did you personally think would make a person say, 'he was going to get you'? Didn't you first tell the police he was a tall light skinned man? What Sarah Hawes did ask was: "How far did he chase you?" and the girl answered, "a couple of feet" and, "did he touch you?" and the girl answered "No," But, both questions tacitly assumed that Charles was the alleged offender. I was aghast at the incompetence. There was no plea, no passion. Daffy Duck could have done a better job.

Judge Bruno considered for about thirty seconds. In his best day, he would never be considered Solomon, but he almost did the right thing. He would throw out those 'listed' charges, because, in light of what actually occurred, they didn't make sense; but, he would find Charles guilty, guilty of ... harassment, and with a bang of the gavel, sentenced him to six months probation and court costs of $150.00 – the bail money his sister put up for his release from jail. I was appalled.

Up until that point I could barely hear the judge, but all at once, he looked at Charles and yelled, *"And if you ever bother this girl again, I'll throw you in jail for a long, long time. Do you understand me?"* Charles was stunned. *"Do you hear me?"* Bruno demanded. It seemed that Charles wanted to say something, but was obeying the PD's warning not to. Charles finally nodded that he heard the judge.

Sarah Hughes came over to me and asked me if I understood what had happened. I told her I did, but she read the unhappy look on my face. She said, "It's a gift, a huge victory, believe me."

As we left the courthouse Charles said, "Well, I guess I got a record now," I nodded in agreement. "I guess it ain't that bad. Almost everybody I know has a record. They could have thrown me in jail. And did you hear the way he yelled at me? Like I was a little boy."

"I guess he thought you did it."

"Yeah. But all he had to do was ask."

"What would you have said if he had?"

"The truth. I would have told him I was totally innocent and he would have realised it too."

"How's that?"

"Because I was on the track team in high school and if I chased a girl down the street I would have caught her."

You could see that he was relieved that it was over. At least he wasn't going to jail. Somehow, his load had been lightened. He shook my hand as we parted. He going his way and I going mine. I watched him briefly as he crossed Vine Street and saw his head start bobbing to a rhythm only he was able to hear. He took out his imaginary sticks and began playing. There was lightness in his step and music in his ear.

Lynne Wycherley

The Whale House
Iceland

Under the rafters their white bones fly.
Their curved shapes carve the air.
Pilot, Bottlenose, Sowerby's, Sei –

labels flutter their moths on wood –
Mincke, Humpback, Cuvier's,
one dry word for countless dead.

I touch history: taste loss.
Sandwhales extinct. We
are architects of an empty house.

Windows frame the landing-quay,
dishonest grey, its memory
washed of blood. If I could I'd play

a Beluga song: how it dives
and soars – plaintive,
exuberant. Outside our sonar

pods fluke, glide, seamless
in their blue element,
more fitted to this watersphere than us.

I catch my breath.
White whales,
dazzling, even in death.

Herring Girl
Lerwick 1920

Exported for summer, I was drunk
with sickness on the Pentland Firth.
The salt wood rose: Women
in tarpaulin, sketched in rows.
A shore swayed its gingery line.
In trios we were sent to our
one-roomed huts, a brown reek
oozing from the curers' yard.

6 am at the pier. Shouts
from the steam-drifters. I wait
by the farlin's gulley, my hands

bandaged against the dancing knife.
Now it fills. Stacked scales. The twitch,
slither, of two thousand fish.
Arms red, sleeves rolled, we
slice the gills, spare the milt.

Our knives work faster than needles.
Fifty a minute: the flesh falls.
Smas, matties, fills. Layer
by filmed layer in a ravenous barrel.
We work in threes, parodies
of the goddess. Later I dream
the moon is a fish, her slit-throat
children staring from steel rivers.

We are the untouchables:
oil stains my skin. Fiddlers
raise a tune. I laugh with the cooper
but his eyes stray seaward.
At night my salt-douched sores
cry red. I slit flour-bags
to bind my fingers, and tighten
the knots with my teeth.

Glacier-walk

We tread on a dome of locked light,
a cyan sun in a perspex shield,
our photo-lenses black against the glare.

Our bones have budded iron –
ice-picks from fists, crampons from feet.
Our hearts quicken as if we are hares.

I lead but you are anchor, ready to weigh
if I fall. Not much rope for a marriage,
they'd say, six metres spanning between us.

If I walk too fast, you drag me back –
too slow, and I might trip you.
We test our steps, cervine,

and inch back from crevasses in our minds:
old cracks of grief where love
might fall and all the world blink out.

Love in the Hebrides

ord

blue mountain-chain,
red ochre sky

spectrum sung
at the world's edge

sgurr bean

i watch your thoughts
skip and pause

mauve footprints
of an arctic hare

Cuilithionn

the mountains rinse
our reflections in water

dark women
washing streaked silk

mingary

will you catch sand
in the marram

of your fingers,
make me a love, a machair?

sligachan

peaks, sheet-mist, white
aquarelle, a world

dissolving backwards
through our hands

Waking to a Storm

In such wind, how can a day begin?
The sky is a carrion crow
rearranging its wings over a disordered nest.

Note that cloud with its angular rain,
goddess stooping with her dark spoon:
there's been a mishap in the kitchen.

Hold tight: light comes in splinters.
Ring-pull, price-tag, fag packet, tin-flash.

Monday, Monday

George Pryde

Monday, and the winter sun casts Joe's shadow along the platform. I turn away from him, gaze across the oil refinery, imagine the two of them together. What would it take? I look down ninety feet to the road.

"You goin out, Willie?" he asks.

"You tellin me?" Joe shrugs, tucks the three-quarter spanner into his belt. "Right, I'll go." He shakes his head. "Got to work you in gently, eh?" It's always there, the needling, the mocking. He winds the rope around his waist, ducks through the platform handrail and lowers himself onto the pipe. He raises his arms to balance and slowly walks six feet to the valve. Only a fool would do this. But then he's doing it for me, parading his contempt. He turns and smiles, sits straddling the pipe with his legs dangling in the air. "Right," he shouts.

I reach out, slowly turn the davit around until the arm is over the valve, with the hook swinging wildly four feet above his head. Once it comes to rest he eases the hook down to about twelve inches above the handwheel. All it would take is a quick turn of the davit and he'd get the hook in his face – an accident that could happen to anyone.

I watch him slip the rope around the valve and up onto the hook, and feel my hands tremble. I grip the handrail to steady myself, and look away, lick my dry lips. Beyond the gaping rust-brown furnaces rising from the mud a dumper truck roars, starts to move. A distant piledriver measures the minutes. Even in this cold I have to wipe the sweat from my brow. Joe's struggling now, cursing.

"Need any help?"

He lifts his head from the valve, disgust on his face, and ignores me. Stretched along the valve, with one grimy fist around the handwheel and his legs wrapped around the pipe, he slackens the flange bolts. Far beneath him, men pour concrete on a bed of steel reinforcing bars.

I spit into the wind, and remember.

"Gie him a bit o authority," Duncan said last Monday, "an he goes aff the heid." He paused. "Honest tae Christ Wullie, ah don't know why you didnae get the job." His huge body spread over the bench, one thick hand splayed across the vice. "Lisa's young, isn't she …? She's a lot younger than you?" He paused again, face flushed. He's a better actor than the rest; you could almost believe his concern, his embarrassment, was real.

"Ay. So what?" Back two weeks and it was starting again. "So what?"

Duncan straightened, loosened his muscles in one circular movement then clamped the small impeller in the vice. He lifted a file and ran it through his fingers.

"Naw … s'nothin … Ah just wondered."

"Wondered what?" I stirred my tea with a chewed pencil, looked up from the mug. "Ah'm *listenin.*"

"Ach, well it's just … he's been sayin things. He's a dirty bastard, ye ken that." Duncan shuffled awkwardly, placed the file on the workbench.

"*What?* Christ, if you've something to say, say it."

Duncan sighed, his eyelids drooping. "S'nothin. Forget it." He looked past me, his eyes restless, scratched his temple. He can spin it out.

I followed the streak of grease on his forehead.

He picked up the file again and lightly trimmed the impeller keyway. "Forget ah ever spoke, Wullie." He rubbed his thigh.

"*Forget!* Bloody finish what you've started … And why you? Why talk to *you* about her?" I'd looked into the big man's eyes, searching for an answer I already knew.

"Don't ask." He paused, looked uneasy. "Ach, Ah'm no up tae that yin. Ah shouldnae've mentioned it."

"Naw, ye shouldnae have. Christ is naebody in this bloody squad goin tae gie me a break?"

"That's no fair. Ah'm only tryin tae – "

"Ay, right." I took a swig of tea, tipped the rest out the window. "Don't kid yersel, ah know what ye're aw daein."

Taking turns to wind me up; a rota for taking the mickey. Joe, Duncan, and Gordon. The Three Stooges. Local men who've worked together for years. Joe taking the lead in everything, pushing at it, going to the limit.

"Is're two horns stickin oot ma heid?" I yelled at Gordon one day as we were dismantling a pump. "Stop starin at me like that, ah know what ah'm doin. What the fuck's wrong, eh? What's fuckin wrong wi me?"

Gordon shrugged, a smile playing on his lips, then he pulled the chain, slowly lifting the cast iron cover from the pump. "Nothin, Wullie, you're imaginin things. Christ you're paranoid, man. See a doctor." Later he told the others how I'd blown it. I'm good for a laugh. Anytime.

"A month's a long time lyin on your back." Duncan blew metal filings from the impeller. He paused, looked at me for a moment before replacing the impeller in the vice.

That said it all. There's a difference between a wind-up and … Truth has a ring to it. I'm no brilliant, but I'm no *that* stupid, either.

Friday evening I went home in the dark to an empty house. I found her sitting out on the patio in the freezing cold, staring into nothing. After a while she turned to me. For an instant she looked like a china doll, dull-eyed and so fragile, so brittle that I felt if I touched her she'd fall apart.

But appearances are deceptive. Couldn't leave a note, she said. Had to tell me to my face. She was leaving. Had enough of my moods, enough of me sleeping the evenings away when I came off shift. There had to be more to life than this. "There's no one else," she insisted. Ay, right.

In this oil refinery, people live in each other's pockets. While I was in hospital Joe called, talked to Lisa, asked after me. "So considerate and kind. He's a real gentleman. I don't know what you've been going on about him for," she said. She was impressed. It shouldn't have surprised me. There's a thing about Joe that gets to some women, and he knows it, plays it for all it's worth.

Now he's huddled over a pipe, ninety feet above the ground, struggling with a rusted bolt, mouthing curses. I turn away, look down on the break tank. Water from the mains supply falls foaming into the tank, exhausts itself on the baffle plates. It rises and settles green and placid around the perimeter. For a minute or two it calms me.

Joe yells into the wind. I ignore him as long as I can, then turn back as he yells again. He's standing on the pipe, both hands around the chain, pulling. The valve rises free of the pipe. The pipe dips a bit under his weight, but not enough. Not enough.

"Right then, Willie, I'm coming back." He sticks the three-quarter spanner into his belt and edges up to the outside of the platform. "Take the spanner," he says, easing it from his belt, don't want to do myself a mischief." He grins. "What would the bints say!" He climbs through the handrail onto the platform and stands, chest heaving. "Right, let's get the valve in," he says, wiping his nose with the back of his hand.

I place the spanner on the platform, turn the davit until the valve is over the railing. Joe sidles past, manhandles the valve into a corner of the platform. When it rests on the grating he slackens the rope, lets the hook swing free. "Got the bonnet spanner?"

I shake my head. I'm tired, so bloody tired, and I've too much on my mind to think about a stupid five-eight bonnet spanner. On Saturday afternoon I dug the hole, had my tea, backfilled with rubble in the dark. Yesterday I poured the concrete base. She'll have a greenhouse.

"Christ, Willie, you know we need a three-quarter spanner *and* a five-eight spanner. How can I get into the valve without the bloody five-eight spanner?" He shakes his head, murmurs, "Jesus!"

"I thought you'd …" The words stick in my throat.

"No, I didn't bring it. You thought wrong." Joe wipes his hands on his overalls, and looks at his watch. "Almost half-twelve. We'll leave it till later." He looks down at the valve and sighs. "Come on, let's get fed." He takes off his hard hat, runs fingers through his hair. "Come on."

I lift the three-quarter spanner from the platform, balance the weight of it in my hand. I stare at the back of Joe's head descending the stairs and feel a dull ache in my body.

He looks back at me, jams the hard hat on his head. "You *comin?*"

I hesitate, drop the three-quarter spanner, kick it aside. Joe shrugs, turns away. I'm shivering as I follow him down. The sun has gone. Mist rises from the river, creeps through the refinery. Condensate from the cooling towers, a great white shroud, drifts over the town.

For an instant I'd lost it, could've killed him. And then … It's too soon for an accident. Nine months, a year, maybe longer. I can wait.

Man and Mule

Angela Howard

At the Verdun Memorial is a glass case containing a mule's hoof, perfectly preserved.
There was once a man who loved his mule. He stabled it in a natural
cave, next to the ammunition store he and his regiment had built
together in the forest behind the fortress.

The man had five mules to look after, and Mule was his favourite.
Mule's hooves never seemed to get dirty like the other mules' hooves did,
though he worked just as hard as the others, pulling the laden carts over
the uneven earth, carrying the regiment's artillery. When the rain slashed
down and flooded the trenches, the other mules would skid; some would
even fall and their fur got caked with mud. Mule seldom fell, and when
he did, he'd just shake his coat and the mud rolled off him. And even
though his feet got wet, the mud always seemed to slip off them, too.

Mule was mute, but you could tell what he was thinking, or at least
what he felt, by the movement of his eyes and the way all his muscles
moved: he loved the man who looked after him. But he couldn't say it;
he wasn't there to say it. He was there to serve, and he served his master
and the regiment well, carrying a ton of danger on his back, making no
sound and no protest as he struggled to follow his master. The other
mules would often stick their feet in the ground and refuse to advance,
swishing their tails, slipping in the mud and starting at the explosions
around them which fell from the sky. But Mule always remained calm.
It wasn't the calm of indifference, though, and the Man loved Mule for
that. Often, after a hard day's work, he'd take much care in varnishing
Mule's hooves with a special brush to enhance the black, white and grey
pattern on the horn, painting every bit of them all the way round to under
the fetlocks. He made Mule's hooves shine. And he did this when the
other mules weren't there so as not to show his preference.

And, out of deference to his master, Mule was careful not to get his
hooves dirty whatever the weather, whatever the constraints, whatever
the long journey, lugging the heavy guns and bombs on his back or
hauling them in the cart behind him. Sometimes when the regiment
ploughed through the large, never-ending muddy fields there'd be
noises ahead of them and men advancing towards them who looked like
his master. But the men wore different metal hats and fired bullets
directly at them so that all the other mules shied and the guns fell off
their backs and the men yelled. However, Mule just stopped and waited
until the Man told him where to go and what to do next.

The Man would unload the bombs off Mule's back, or off the cart, and
hand them over to the regiment soldiers who shot the bombs up in the
air towards the men opposite, where they exploded. The noise was ear-

splitting. Things came falling out of the air, landing with a bang around Mule and the regiment. But Mule didn't budge; he watched it all happen, or rather he watched how his master handled the explosives, how he handed out the gas masks to everyone, sometimes fixing special masks on Mule and the other mules, too. He stood still throughout the battle, waiting silently for the Man to finish his duty and come back to him, while the other mules reared and kicked out, swirled round and round, straining their harness, trying to break free from their carts with the wheels stuck in the mud.

One day – it was after the rain – when they arrived back at the fortress and when the Man started to unload Mule's cart, stacking the heavy guns and bombs in the cave, there was a sudden explosion. Everyone was blasted against the fortress wall and pieces of iron, stone and metal shot up in the air into a cloud of flying debris. And then it all fell, and when at last it had all settled, everything was silent. There was a mountain of smoking rubble, ruin and mud in the middle of the courtyard. Everything was grey; grey dust vanishing into grey slush. Even the sky was grey, and the silence was stronger than Mule's.

Mule had been blown to pieces. He'd been standing in the yard, waiting for the Man to come back to him. The Man was alive, though, as were the other mules, and all the soldiers of the regiment.

The others lay in their bunks exhausted, but the Man stayed up all night in the rain, searching in the debris with his torch, turning over the bits and pieces of iron, the shattered stone, the shrapnel and the mud.

He found Mule's leg just before dawn, and picked it up, took it into the cave and sat in a corner with it, wiping it with a chamois leather, even though there wasn't much dirt on it. Nor was there any sign of blood. Perhaps the rain had washed it away.

But perhaps it hadn't. He thought for a moment, and then took out his varnish and brush and started to paint Mule's hoof again, using precise, downward strokes with the brush, and as he did so found himself thinking about Mule's character, – his spirit, for want of a better word – and where it could be now, what it was, exactly. He surprised himself thinking like this, and stopped for a moment, brush in hand. Because never before in his life had he thought such things, about spirits, or whatever it was Mule had left behind inside the Man.

He waited for the varnish to dry, then took out his comb and ran it carefully and slowly through the light-brown fur, remembering the feel of Mule's docile obedience, the nudge of his muzzle under his arm. He smoothed the coat down so it lay neatly over the top part of the hoof which shone beautifully with the varnish, more so than it had ever done before. Then he went searching for a strip of leather and found Mule's saddle strung up on a branch overhanging the cave.

This made him realise just how big the explosion had been. Perhaps that's what it takes to make one wake up. He began to tremble inside, something he'd never done before. Before, everything had been exploding outside him, around him, but now it was inside him, opening doors he didn't know existed, onto things he'd never seen before.

He cut a strip from Mule's saddle and stretched it over the top of the severed limb and sewed it into the skin to protect the open bit at the top, then stepped outside clutching Mule's hoof and took a piece of shrapnel which lay in the mud by the entrance. The Captain was there and was saying something about how lucky they'd been not losing any of their men, but that they'd better check in case there was a dead body in the wreckage from another regiment or indeed from the enemy camp. But the Man didn't hear.

Because not everyone listens to what they hear. But the man needed to put into words what he felt, so he scratched into the leather at the top of the hoof. The piece of shrapnel was a crude instrument to write with, so all he could put was: "Faithful Mule. Verdun 1916".

Then he turned back to his other mules. The Captain was ordering everyone else to clear the yard. "There may be an enemy body in there. Find it. You too." He pointed to the Man.

The Man obeyed.

Comet

I pruned the roses, dug up roots
hacked down trees, raked the earth,
scalped the land, couldn't go far enough
        While you stood still

You said I was mad, I dug harder
cut through horizons, swept all clean
left you behind
        on Earth.

The view of Earth is blurred from up here
like silver through frost of the breath I blew.
Up here all is clear, there is rock and ravine
smooth-clean, the ground is hard
there is shadow and light I could cut with a knife
        but I won't.

Occasionally I have a fleeting visitor
his mane is on fire, he is in a hurry
I watch his trail vanish but he will be back
in the same fury, over and over
and over again.
        I prefer it like that.

Star

It fell at night by the side of a tree
seared a hole through a drying leaf
flashed its light back up to the sky
where life spins on without stopping.

It sank back and faded, winter came
forced it to hibernate. I picked it up,
rubbed it alive, ran home clutching it
my husband sat up, dropping his book

"What has happened?" he said.
"You have light in your eyes."
And his eyes don't leave me
they'd never really seen me before.

It nestles in my chest, the tiny pulse
of the tiny child we never had.
"I see light there inside you." He walks towards me,
eyes fixed on my chest. I clutch at my star

as he lays me down in the wintry leaves.
But the chill of years, unspent in desiring,
brushes over our nakedness and
my star spins back to its life in the sky.

Guantanamo

Like a cheetah shackled in a cage
he pads a network of revenge
mapping out the lands he'll conquer
once the bolts are loosened.

Before, he had no particular purpose
but new spots reveal the quarrel
raging underneath.
How he'll run wild once he's set free
racing across Savannah'd worlds
North, South, East, West,

eyes surveying, spreading rebellion
shoulders peaked,
jagged, like the mountain range
where underneath in a sand-dried den
his rebel leader snarls honeyspun words
fuelling hatred beyond horizons.

The Heichts o Macchu Picchu

Set owre frae Pablo Neruda's 'Alturas de Macchu Picchu'

John Law

I

Frae air intil air, lik a tuim net,
I wis vaigin streets an souch,
comin in by, or thonner awa fareweel –
come hairst – til the hansel o siller
in the leafs – an atween ware an corn-heids –
til whit fulness luve, lik whit's intil a gluve
faain, fees til us lik a free-haundit muin.

(Days o lifesome brichtness in the steer
o boadies, steels transmutit,
hauden til thair wheesht in vitriol:
nichts pistelt til hinmaist flour:
duntit stamens o the mairriet airt.)

A bodie bydin for me amang the fiddles
trystit wi a warld lik a yirdit touer
dreelin its screw stair deeper nor aa
the leafs the colour o lode sulphur:
an laicher yit, in geologic gowd
lik sweird scabbardit in meteors
I doukit the haun, disorderly an douce,
fouterin wi the yirth's ain quim.

I boued the pow fornent profoond swaw,
plunkit lik smaa drap in sulphuric dwaam,
an, blinnd man me, gaed back the jasmine yett
til worn oot ware-time o humanity.

II

Gin flouer til flouer skies aa its seed
an the rock hauds hits flouer seminate
in buskin wrocht o diamant an saun,
man's aye ruggin the florish o the licht he wales
frae the weirdit wal-springs o the seas
an dreels the metal dirlin in his neives.
Suin, amang the claes an smeik, aa ower the spulyied brode
lik a shauchle o cairds, the sowl hunkers:
quartz an waukrifeness, tears grat in ocean
maks stanks o cuilth: but aye an on

fowk murders it, manks it wi blads an wi haterent,
smoors it in the hap o the daily-day, rives it
atour thae cleuk razzors cleidin the wire.

Nae wey: sen in corridors, luft, at sea, on hieweys
wha, lik the poppies incarnadine, gets roadit
wi nae knife ti hain his bluid? Angir haes skailt that
o the puir gear o the troker in fowk;
the whyle, at the heichts o the bolas tree preins
the dew hits claer caird a thousan year aareadies
til the samen trystin tweig. Och hert, och face,
grund fine intil cavernous howes o hairst.

Hou monie time in hibernal vennels o the muckle toun, or on
the bus, or a boat at gloamin, or i thon grossest laneheid
nicht o feis or fair, droukit i the soond o bells an scaddas
fair in the vault o human pleisour
wis I waantin ti haud back an leuk
for the ayebydin threid sae ill ti finnd
I haed fummelt at the ainct in stane
or i the refulgence at a bosie gied us.

(As wi the wey wi grain lik tellin owre gowd
the smaa swalmin breists wisna ti coont
an thaim aye sae braw in first buskin
an at, aye peels, huils til ivory;
sae wi whaur the watters o hame rises for shuir,
dirlin frae faur-aff snaws til bluid-dibbelt waves.)

Me, I cuid juist aboot haud on til a clanjamphrie o faces an masks
cuissen doun lik boss rings o gowd
lik duds o hallierackit dochters o a rabid hairst
shakkin the mankit tree o the fleggit fowk.

Wisna steid whaur haun o mine micht rest
nor onie bit rinnin lik yokit watters
siccar as nugget o coal or chrystal
warmin het or cauld til ma apen haun.

Whit like wis fowk? In whitna bit o thair dailygaun blethers
amang thair mercats an thair whustlins-oot –
in whitna metal o thair muvements
bade thair unbrekkable, daithless, gust o life?

III

Veive beins lik mealies fell incalculate skails
in the staved girnel o willsome actions, waefu haps
frae ane til seiven or eicht-fauld;
an no the ae daith kythed, but monie til ilkane,
a wee daith ilka day, stour, maggot, leerie
drouned in the dub o suburbs, a peerie daith wi creeshie weings
penetratit ilk man lik a cuttie pike
investin him wi breid or blade:
the drover, son o herbours, the daurk captain o pleuchs
the roddan, stravaiger o thrang vennels:
the haill o them enfaibelt, bydin on daith, belyve an daily-day
thair daurklin in dwyne o drow ilka day
a bleck tassie trimmlin in thair hauns as thay tuimed it.

IV

Michtiest daith invitit me monie time
he wis lik saut dernit in the swaw
an whit his unseen saur seedit
wis hauf-roads deeps, hauf-roads heichts
or huge constructs o wind an snaw-huird.

I cam til the airn rig, til the kyles o
atmosphere, til the mortclaith o ferm an stane
til the tuim starn slaps o hinmaist steps
an the heid-birlin turnpike pad:
yit, braid sea, o daith! No wave bi wave div ye win til us
but suddent-like wi a spunder o daurk certainty,
lik a wrocht-oot calculus o nicht.

Ye neiver cam rypin throu pooches, nor wadna
cry in athout ye war cleidit aa in rid,
haudin yer wheesht in a carpet o dawin,
in hie an yirdit heirskeps o tears.

I cuidna loe in ilka bodie's ain sel
thon tree boukit wi aa its bygane back-ens
(the daith o a thousan blads)
aa the fause daiths an resurrections
but grund, but depth:
I weished ti drouk masel in the fuhlest lives
in the braidest firths
an whan, bit bi bit, man cam barrin me oot
steikin his pads an duirs fornent me, I cuidna rax
wi ma streamin hauns his herriet inexistence;

I gaed syne street bi street, reiver bi reiver,
ceitie bi ceitie, bed efter bed,
atour deserts ma sautie visor steered,
an amang the endmaist howffs, wantin leerie, wantin fire
breid, stane, seilence, I vaigit ma lane
deein o ma ain daith.

V

It wisna yersel, dour daith, steel-pennit gled,
that the puir heritor in sicna hooses heftit
kirned in a tuim crap wi his gorbelt fuid –
but raither, a bit wrack o auld duin raip,
a souch o bravery that didna pruve,
or some wersh dew cuidna brak sweit.
It wis whit canna be born owre, a crottle
o peerie daith but paece or beild:
a bane, a bell, that wis deein intil him.
I liftit the iodine haps on ma hauns
an doukit them deep in wee pains wad smoored daith
an naething fand amang the lesion but cauld blasts o win
that jeeled the tuim slaps o ma sowl.

VI

Sclimmin bi the steps o the yirth syne
throu the jaggy stent o the jungil wids
ti meet yersel, Macchu Picchu.
Hie ceitie o steppit stanes
lang hame o whitna yirth
wis neiver seen in nichtgoun hiddlins.
As wi sib faimlies o the samen weird
you trystit whaur the crib o licht an man
dannelt in a win o jags.

Mither o stane, condor spunk.

Hie brig o man at his dawin.

Spad yirdit in the firsten saun.

This wis the beild, this is the steid:
here the sapsie maize mealies shot up
ti skail in season again lik rid hailstanes.

Cairdit here the vicuna's gilten threid
Luvers ti cleid, thair graves, thair mithers,
the keing, the prayin fowk, the sodgers.

An up by here the feet o men fand peace bi nicht
nearhaun the cleuks o aigles
in thair maet-stappit nests, an at the daw
thay sallied oot wi dunnerin feet amang the liftin haar
preein yirth an stane ti ken
thair wey again come nicht, come daith.

Mervellin on cleidin an hauns,
the touk o watter in the cistern's soondin howe,
the waa leam-smuithed bi the bosie o a face
that wi ma ain een saw the lichts o yirth ablo
eylin wi ma ain hauns the timmers gane nou,
for at aathing: cleidin, ledder, pats, palaver,
wine an breid is wede awa, caaed til yirth.

In cam the souch syne wi its fingirs
lik the flouers o lemons dawtin the sleepin fowk:
a thousan year o souch, months an weeks o it,
a blae win aff airn rigs o bens
cam in aboot wi dentie typhoon feet
ti sloonge the lanesome closes o the stane.

VII

You indwallin deid o ae abyss, scaddas o ae ravine,
profoondest, as ti pynt bi compass
the maik o yer magnitude
I see hou it breardit, thon back end o daith
frae ootmined rocks
frae capitals o crammasie
frae aqueducts in spate
ye tummelt heidlang at the hairst
til thon singil yirdin.
Nae mair the day the tuim air murns
nor kens yer feet, glaurie wi cley,
myndsna in whitten pats ye syndit the luft
the time gullies o lichtnin ryved its harigals
an etten bi haar the michty
tree wis felled bi the blast.

It hained a haun that raxit suddent
frae croun til ruit o time.
Ye'r perished aa an haill: ettercap fingirs, frail
threids, raivelt claith – aathing ye war
caaed doun: hants an hyne-awa utterance,
the glentin masks o licht.

Leuk at me frae the foonds o the yirth
plouer o paurks, wyver, quate hird:
groom o guairdian llamas:
mason hie on yer coggly scaffle:
you, sellin the watter the Andes grat:
gowdsmith wi warkin fingirs:
fashed fermer at the seedlins:
patter waured at the weare:
brim the tassie o this new life
wi yer auld yirdit sorras.
Shaw me yer bluid an the dreel ye drave;
tell me: here whaur the whup peyed ye
for at a gemstane didna skinkle or the yirth
wadna lowss swith its stent o corn or stane:
pynt oot ti me the boolder whaur ye stummelt,
the timmer thay crucified ye wi,
scart auld flint til tindle an pit lowe
til auncient leeries, shaw furth the whup-strauns
tangit intil yer wounds age efter age,
the aixes lustrous wi yer bluid.

I come ti gie tongue til yer deid vyces.

Atour the yirth forgaither aa
the seilent nithert lips
oot o the deeps speak yer stories this lang nicht
as tho we bade at anchor here, babbin thegither.

An lat me ken aathing, chainyie on chainyie,
link bi link an step bi step;
sherpen the gullies ye haed haen in hiddlins awa,
hilt them in ma breist, throu ma hauns,
lik an onding o solar radiance,
lik a spate o beeriet jaguars,
an lae me greetin: oors, days, years,
blinnd ages, centuries o starns.

An gie me the seilence, the watter, the howp.

Gie me the struissle, the airn, the volcanoes.

Lat me staun lodesman for the deid.

Speak for yersels throu ma vyce, ma bluid.

divvied up amang its glacier greetin,
sheuk neive amang its swack sweirds –
pummelt its weir-reft stamens –
bure on til its sodger's beild,
blaffin til its weird in craigs?

Whit whusperins in yer haikit leamins?
Did yer secret rebel sklent
gang fuit-lowss, thrang wi message?
Whit ane dauners furth, crumpin cranreuch syllables,
bleck eidioms, flags o gowd,
faddomless vyces an thrappelt yowts
in yer sclender arteirs o watter?

Whit ane gangs sneddin the floral eelids
that comes ti ponder us frae the mouls?
Whit ane's chuckin the deid castocks doun
that skails frae yer hauns in a spate
ti thrash intil a coal seam in geology
in thair thrashen-oot nicht?

Wha cuttit the linkin tree?
Wha's aye yirdin fareweels?

Luve, luve, dinna gang near the mairches,
dinna be browdent on this sunken heid:
lat time tak its ful meisure
in its chawmer o fruschit walsprings –
here, atween torrents an craigs,
tak you the souch o the bealachs,
the laminatit parallels o the wind,
the blinnd canal o the cordilleras,
the soor walcome o the dew,
an sclim, flouer bi flouer, throu densities,
strample the serpent cuissen doun.

In this airt o escarpments, stanes an wids,
stour o green starns, jungil-clear,
the strath o Mantur kythes lik a leivin loch
or a new storey o seilence.

Come til ma ain sel, til ma ain dawin
Up til the crounin laneheid.

The deid kinrik bydes on yit.

An atour the Sundial the daurk scadda
o the condor cruises lik a sail o black.

IX

Aigle atween starns, vine i the haar.
Forlatten dun, blinnd scimitar.
Belt o Orion, breid transubstantiate.
Stair o stair-rod rain, etin ee-lid.
Jib-sail o cleidin, stane pollen.
Lowe o granite, stane breid.
Serpent o meinerals, stane rose.
Boat-beirial, foont o stane.
Muin horse, licht o stane.
Equinox quadrant, vapour o stane.
Endmaist Euclidean, beuk o stane.
Iceberg wrocht in the storms.
Coral o time drouned.
Fingir-saftent mantle.
Feddir-battert ruif.
Mirror sclenters, foonds o thunners.
Thrones mankit bi speilin vine.
Law o the bluidie cleuk.
Blast steyed on the brae.
Blae frozen watterfaa.
Bells o the sleepin forefowk.
Habble o hauden-doun snaws.
Airn bunden on statuary.
Hersh wather sneckit ayont rax.
Pads o puma, bluidstane.
Touerin scadda, communin o snaw.
Nicht hystit wi fingirs an ruits.
Windae o the mists, hertless doo.
Fulyerie o nicht, avatar o thunner.
Rigbane o bens, swaws' ruif.
Biggins o aigles faur astray.
Luft raip, mairch-line o the bee.
Bluid ee-line, starn wrocht.
Beilin o meineral, quartz muin.
Snake o the Andes, pow o amaranth.
Seilent cupola, sained mitherland.
Sea wife, intimmers o cathedral.
Bou o saut, bleck-weingit gean.
Teeth snaw-crouned, cauld thunner.
Mankit muin, ill-feyin stane.
Birse o the cauld, rub o the win.
Volcano haun-heizit, daurklin breenge.
Siller swaw, flane o weird.

X

Stane aye upon ither, an whaur wis Man intil't?
Air intil air, an whaur wis Man intil't?
Time efter time, an whaur wis Man intil't?
Wis you the brukken bit yersel
o Man unfree, tuim gled
that throu the day's causey, bi the auld gates,
throu the leafs o deid hairsts
gangs fleitchin at the sowl for a yirdin?
Puir haun an fit, an puir auld life itsel –
thae days o naukit licht in yersel,
onding kenspeckle faain on feires
at the feis, gang tell us wis thay meat til ye,
petal bi daurk petal intil siccan a tuim gub?
Hungir, mankind's coral
hungir, herb in hiddlins, ruit o the hewers o wid,
hungir, did ye hull the boatie thay wis sailin
by thae hie an whit wanchancie touers?

I'm speirin at you, saut o the hie roads,
shaw's the trouel; lat me, biggins,
grinnd stane stamens wi a staff,
sclim ilka step o air til vacuum,
howk in the wame til I finnd man.
Macchu Picchu, did ye pit
stane upon stane, an the foond, fowks' duds?
Coal upon coal, on a bed o tears?
Fire on the gowd, an athin it trimmlin, the rid
jaup o bluid?

Gie me back the thirlbun ye yirdit!
Shak frae the yirth the bannocks
o the puir, shaw me the bansman's
cleidin an his windae,
whit like he sleepit whyle he leived.
An gin he sleepit
snoiterin, gantin lik a bleck howe
howkit in the waa, that taivert.
The waa, the waa! Gin ilka coorse o stane
wechtit doun his sleep, an gin he fell ablo
as unner a haill muin, sleepin!

Auld America, drount bride,
your fingirs an aa,
flittin the jungil for the tuim heichts o the gods

unner mairriage banners o licht an piety,
mellin wi thunner frae the drums an lances,
yours, your fingirs an aa,
thaim that the abstract rose an the rig o cauld, thaim
that the bluidstained corp o the new corn bure
til a wab o glaizie stuff, til the hardent howes,
did ye hain, did ye, beiriet America, in the muckle howe
o yer soor harigals, lik an aigle, hungir?

XI

Throu spulyie o splendour
nicht wrocht in stane, lat me douk ma haun
an gar gaun pulse in masel, lik bird jylt a thousan year
the auld forlatten hert.
Mynd me nane cantieness the day, braider nor the sea,
for that man is braider yit nor sea nor onie braid o islands
an we maun dern oorsels in him lik a wal ti draa oot
secret watters an subtle truiths.
Lat me na mynd, stane circle, the wechtie shapes,
the ower-airchin spreid, hinney-caim's riggin,
an aff the square lat ma haun sweel doun
the hypotenuse o hair sark an saut bluid.

Whan in the orderin o its flicht the heid-batterin condor dunts
ma pow, horseshae-haurd as duin weing-cases,
an his hurricane o sanguinary fedders steers the daurk stour
doun sclentin stairweys, I dinna see the raptor's onset
dinna see the blinnd heuk o his cleuks –
I see the auld bodie, the bondsman, the sleeper
in the paurks, I see a cheil, a thousan cheils, a man, a thousan wemen
droukit in the bleck onding, brunt bleck wi rain an nicht
livid an staned wi statues' wecht
Johnnie mac a'Chlachair, son o Wiracocho
Johnnie Cauldwame, aff the green starn,
Johnnie Barfuit, graunwean til the turquoise
come rise wi me an be born aa, ma brithers.

XII

Up wi me, brither, an be born.

Gie me yer haun oot the deep airts
Set wi yer sadness.
Nae mair foriver frae thir craigs.
Nae mair foriver frae time's yirdin.
Yer raucle vyce nae mair foriver.
The glent winna return til yer pykit-oot een.

X

Stane aye upon ither, an whaur wis Man intil't?
Air intil air, an whaur wis Man intil't?
Time efter time, an whaur wis Man intil't?
Wis you the brukken bit yersel
o Man unfree, tuim gled
that throu the day's causey, bi the auld gates,
throu the leafs o deid hairsts
gangs fleitchin at the sowl for a yirdin?
Puir haun an fit, an puir auld life itsel –
thae days o naukit licht in yersel,
onding kenspeckle faain on feires
at the feis, gang tell us wis thay meat til ye,
petal bi daurk petal intil siccan a tuim gub?
Hungir, mankind's coral
hungir, herb in hiddlins, ruit o the hewers o wid,
hungir, did ye hull the boatie thay wis sailin
by thae hie an whit wanchancie touers?

I'm speirin at you, saut o the hie roads,
shaw's the trouel; lat me, biggins,
grinnd stane stamens wi a staff,
sclim ilka step o air til vacuum,
howk in the wame til I finnd man.
Macchu Picchu, did ye pit
stane upon stane, an the foond, fowks' duds?
Coal upon coal, on a bed o tears?
Fire on the gowd, an athin it trimmlin, the rid
jaup o bluid?

Gie me back the thirlbun ye yirdit!
Shak frae the yirth the bannocks
o the puir, shaw me the bansman's
cleidin an his windae,
whit like he sleepit whyle he leived.
An gin he sleepit
snoiterin, gantin lik a bleck howe
howkit in the waa, that taivert.
The waa, the waa! Gin ilka coorse o stane
wechtit doun his sleep, an gin he fell ablo
as unner a haill muin, sleepin!

Auld America, drount bride,
your fingirs an aa,
flittin the jungil for the tuim heichts o the gods

On the Edge

Peter Bromley

The man on the television was crying, his turban coming loose, his lined face, large and tanned, set against a background of pale mountains. The camera panned back to show him holding the body of a child as he explained that his own countrymen had attacked his village with gas. His eyes flicked like those of a trapped animal. He wanted someone to help him understand. I watched footage of dead mothers and fathers lying over the bodies of children they'd tried to protect from the invisible cloud. When the camera cut back to the man, he started to cry. He moaned, rocking backwards and forwards with grief as he explained he had been at market in a distant town, so missing the attack. He said that he wished he was also dead, then stared silently at the camera, waiting.

They radioed me to say a storm was coming and that they were worried about me. I said I knew about the storm. I'd seen the weather forecasts they emailed me. It was my job to know about the storm.

"I'm OK!" I said.

"But you're on your own."

"I volunteered to be here."

"That's not the point."

"I'll survive."

"I'm sure you will."

I turned to watch the gannets through the window – large, awkward birds on land, but in water, powerful and perfectly shaped – pure white knives cutting silently into the ocean. They rarely come ashore, except for breeding. when they use rocky outcrops like this. From the lighthouse I could see them on the rock and also far out to sea in search of food.

The man was on TV again. News broadcasts carried his picture and those of the dead villagers. The scenes were now padded out with maps and long-distance shots of surrounding mountains, but the man and his son remained at the core of the broadcast. He looked old, but was probably no older than me. Some front teeth were missing, and he had a deeply wrinkled face. There was a cut above one eye, but the roughness of the scab didn't look too different from the rest of his skin. He stared intently at the camera as tears ran down his cheeks; only when the camera panned down to take a shot of the son did his head move to look at the small, limp bundle. He was lying flopped across his father's arms. One of his legs dangled free, a rough dusty sandal on his foot; his red and green shirt and loose red cotton trousers flapped gently in the air. The man blinked against the sun. He ended in silence, staring at the interviewer before turning to walk away from the camera, back into the house behind him.

Between writing my reports in the silence of my glass world and the television, I watched the birds through my small, round windows, binoculars by my side which I used to follow birds many kilometres out to sea, watching white splashes appear on the surface as each bird dived into the swell. They were more active than ever; the young birds were growing up and getting ready to leave. There is usually a lot of activity in the colony, but this was becoming intense. Adult birds flew to find ever-increasing amounts of food for their young, spending all day out at sea, diving, flying, diving, flying. Then one day they would be gone … North Africa, The Bay of Biscay, Iceland – places I have only ever seen on maps.

On the rock, the gannets and kittiwakes began to settle down to sit out the storm. There was less flying out to sea. Instead, they sat quietly and began to await the inevitable, squeezing into small cracks and crevices to afford themselves a little protection. The adults still tried to give their young some warmth by wrapping their wings around them.

A few days ago, I saw a Roseate Tern. It just stopped for a rest then was gone. God alone knows how far it had flown or where it was going. This island is not on its usual migratory route. My book described it as a rare visitor to these coastal areas. So what drove a thing so small and delicate to this rock? What lay in its sharp skulls and behind its pin-bright eyes? It was sitting on the rail around the upper light and I simply moved across the window and it was gone. Presumably it had been knocked off course by the storm. But as the clouds gathered on the distant horizon it headed back towards them and the advancing veils and curtains of rain.

At school I listened only occasionally to the teacher, Mr McDermott, when he told us about birds and wildlife. I would walk to school along the rough road and pay more attention to my games than the wildlife around me. Once Megan Leary pointed to a bird that was singing as it ascended in a series of bursts.

"There's a skylark," she said.

"Here's a right lark," I said, pushing her.

Megan married Declan and moved away from the area before I did.

In my class at school, Mr McDermott had better stories to tell. He told us about the Island of St Kilda. The children in my class were of different ages – it was only a small village school. He showed us a map of Scotland, pointing to somewhere out in the middle of the Atlantic – or so it seemed. Then he told us about the people who used to live there: Primitive and God-fearing, he called them. I loved that phrase. He told us how they were removed from their homes and the island became a military base, how they used to send and receive mail in a wooden box attached to an inflated sheep's bladder. The young men would climb cliffs in bare feet to get gull and kittiwake eggs for food. But first they had to show their bravery by standing at the edge of a towering granite ledge in bare feet. Then they had to stand with only their heels on the rock, and finally with only one heel on the rock, the other leg and foot wavering out over the distant sea. Mr McDermott showed us photographs of St Kilda people, small, almost fat, perhaps cause of all the thick clothing they had to wear. Their beards were rough and unkempt. "Primitive and God-fearing".

On the way home from school, Megan, her brother, James and I played at being on St Kilda. James took off his shoes and tried to balance on one of his father's farm walls. At first he couldn't balance on the rough granite blocks of the wall, but eventually he edged his toes out over the fresh air. With time, as the dusk drew in around us, he managed to balance on one heel, his foot half on and half off the wall. I couldn't do it and neither could Megan, who was younger than us both. I satisfied myself by thinking that James wouldn't have been able to balance on the rocks had they been a hundred metres high and not just one metre. As we walked to our respective homes, in the gloom I heard James shout: "King of St Kilda."

The man appeared on TV again. The images hardly varied. Occasionally the order changed, but the same message came across; he was at market so he missed the gas attack but all his family was killed, including his three-year-old son. He wished he was also dead. Some images, like these, come to represent entire episodes of life, like the picture of the young naked girl running away from the bombing in the Vietnam War. Or the loyalist soldier shot during the Spanish Civil War, his arms outstretched as if being crucified. Sometimes we live through important times.

There was worldwide reaction to the gassing. In a far-away building, the Ambassador of the man's country at the United Nations denied the gas attack and blamed the deaths on The Hand of God. He was surrounded by TV cameras, microphones and jostling angry people. Outside the UN building a crowd was waving banners and placards. The man's role was reduced to a small cameo; we saw his tears and his dead child, but now we were seeing other dead mothers and fathers and their children who must have fallen just where they were when the gas hit them and only a few parents had been able to cover them. Some groups of bodies lay next to games or books spread out on the dirt road outside the houses. Others were in the corners of courtyards around unfinished meals. The people from outlying villages arrived to bury relatives and friends. Those that had not been buried were covered with blankets. And still the man came onto each broadcast, crying and wishing he were dead.

I ventured out onto the rock – I did try to get out at least once each day. Walking carefully among the birds not to disturb them, I passed through a slowly moving lawn of white, like a silk sheet rippling. The birds simply ruffled their feathers and fidgeted on their rough nesting mounds. I walked to the end of the rock and looked over to the west. Above the horizon were the first few clouds of the leading edge of the storm that knocked the tern off course as it tried to find directions in the maelstrom. In the evening glow I tried to bring myself to stand on the edge of the rock, toes out over the ocean. Below me was a ten-metre drop into the water. I didn't do it, but turned and walked back through the birds.

When I returned to the lighthouse the radio was crackling.

"Where have you been?" asked the voice.

"Nowhere."

"We've been trying for ten minutes."

"Sorry."

"Shall we come and get you."

"No. I'm fine."

Next morning, I went through my routine, checking the systems. The radio receiver I was upgrading was to be controlled by a single computer; one station would handle over fifteen lights along this coast. I just needed to be present as it was re-tested. As the first specks of rain began to fall I went down the steps, out onto the rock. The birds were preparing to meet the storm head on, the younger birds protected by their parents while older chicks settled down alongside the adults. About half way along the rock the wind and rain hit hard. I looked over the colony to see the birds squatting and crouching close to the rock and turned round to return to shelter. Back in my office, I watched them through the window.

Mr McDermott told us of the storms on St Kilda, how the boats could not put to sea for weeks, sometimes months. The whole Atlantic Ocean would seem to hurl itself at the small granite island and the islanders could only sit and wait. He told how herds of sheep were moved from island to island to graze the scarce grass. During storms the sheep could die of starvation if left for too long on small islands where there was too little food. or be washed away by large waves and their bodies would float, rotting and bloated, between the islands. The storms, he said, were the reasons the Authorities gave for removing the people. But he said it was really because they wanted the island for a military base. So Mr McDermott's grandparents were shipped off the island and given a home in Glasgow. He had a photograph of the tall tenement block where his ancestors lived and, only five months after leaving St Kilda, died.

"They couldn't take it, you see," he said, as we stared at the crumpled photo. "And I end up teaching you lot," he would say, smiling again. At the end of each term, as a special treat, he would tell us stories of St Kilda.

Through the storm the television images moved on. They still showed the man, but also villagers from surrounding areas packing up their belongings and moving down the hillside to the rocky valley floor. They said they were moving together for safety. They sat in family groups in the bare countryside. Tents were flown in from around the world and they clung, with their occupants, to the rocks and scree. Primitive and God-fearing people. The storm raged outside, silencing the man's sorrow. The hills where the people gathered were bare and dusty and the sun cast deep shadows in the valleys. The people sat motionless on the pale stones as cameras panned across their faces. The reporter stood facing the camera to tell us that the refugees would need to be moved to safer, more suitable ground as the mountains could not sustain them for very long; the valleys were inaccessible for the rescue services and international aid. And, finally, the man appeared again, holding the body of his young son.

I looked out again onto the rock below. Groups of birds were bedraggled and weather-beaten, lying crouched together with the young moving as close to their parents as possible. I watched both the television and the storm until the rain and wind finally abated, then went down the steps and onto the shining rock. Many birds were badly injured, a lot were dead. Others were just in shock. But already they were starting to get on with their lives. Some were flying off to sea to seek food for their young.

I stared down into the muddied waters. The storm had stirred up sand and seaweed, clouding the normally-clear sea. It moved aggressively below. I sat on the edge, feet dangling into space beneath, moving my legs from side to side to the rhythm of the waves, tapping my heels against the rock. Eventually I stood up, took off my shoes and moved towards the edge of the cliff, shuffling a few centimetres at a time until my toes were at the absolute edge of the rock, manoeuvring my feet timidly until the toes were over the edge. At last half of each foot was sticking out over the rock. Then I lifted one foot and stretched it out in front of me, standing with only one heel on the rock with the rest of me suspended in space over the sea. I looked to the horizon where the storm came from, and at the confusion and sorrow around me in the colony, until my calf-muscles ached. Then, I edged back, put my shoes and socks on. The birds were quite still and subdued. Back in the lighthouse I answered the radio.

"We're coming to get you."

"I'm all right."

"We're coming to get you. How are things?"

"Nothing changes."

"We will send a boat."

"I'm not going anywhere," I said.

So now, for the last time, I sit at my desk and watch the birds through the small window. More are venturing out to sea again. I follow them through my binoculars. And there are birds still sitting on their nest sites, some injured, some killed by the storm, their bodies in strange, contorted shapes, necks badly twisted. I think to myself: 'The Hand of God'.

Periodically I turn my binoculars on the headland. A boat emerges from behind it. Beyond it, and oddly out of proportion because of the binoculars, rises the cliff, thirty, forty, fifty metres vertically. I imagine myself standing barefoot at the top of that cliff: The King of St Kilda.

The boat moves slowly through the open water. It will take an hour and a half, possibly two, to reach me. It moves carefully through the swell, still high after the winds. Once clear of the cliffs, it turns towards the lighthouse, towards the island and the calm which now envelopes it.

The Emotional Charge of Art

Don McNeil

A mature student from Glasgow School of Art stood in my studio recently, surrounded by my paintings. She expressed delight and excitement but I was stunned when she told me one of her tutors maintained there was no room for emotion in today's art! That set me reflecting on my time at Glasgow School of Art in the early 60s. I was fortunate in being taught not just to draw, but also to see.

I was lucky to learn from a established artists including David Donaldson, Sinclair Thomson, William Armour and Geoff Squires and up-and-coming practitioners like Duncan Shanks and George Devlin. They were all inspirational, and not only in the most obvious way. I recall being set a still life by Willie Armour, Head of Drawing and Painting. He took the morning class, and in the afternoon we were taught by Duncan Shanks who had just graduated and was working as a visiting tutor.

When Willie saw my picture, he wanted me to tone down the oranges. I did so, but seeing the dull oranges that afternoon Duncan said, "Make the oranges sing …" I hastily squeezed out the thick juicy oil paint but next morning was reprimanded by Willie for not doing as I was told! This pattern continued for a few days before I realised I would need to paint separate pictures for Willie and for Duncan. However, this exchange taught me one important lesson. You don't paint for other people – you paint for yourself. Sadly, in today's terms a large number of artists don't paint for themselves – they paint for the cash register.

After leaving art school I went to Jordanhill. After six months I was released to work with youngsters whom I was determined to make love art as passionately as I did. Thirty years later I finally admitted defeat.

By that time it was obvious that the educational establishment was ignorant of the importance of developing creative skills in *all* youngsters. So the majority of pupils who should and could have been inspired and changed by art instead were allowed, indeed encouraged to see the study of art as a waste of time. In addition those in charge now maintained that the 'process' was more important than the 'finished' piece. That meant, amongst other things, that the subject was forced to take on the computer – which, I felt, devalued the role of the art teacher and art itself.

My chance to leave this changed and debased profession came when the Tory Government, keen to save money, offered early retirement to teachers over 50 in promoted posts. Then I moved to Newton with my partner and now wife, Jean Bell, also a painter. For the last ten years we have run Fyne Studios – the Hidden Gallery as we call it – set in an idyllic small village on the shores of Loch Fyne. We also hold weekly classes.

These are immensely rewarding; our style of teaching is appreciated, and understood. One student is the writer Mike Russell. In a recent column for the *Times Educational Supplement* he described his experience of learning art at school. contrasting it with our classes, observing that "slowly, and without realising ... I was being taught", and noting that "for Don and Jean, art is a passion they wish to share".

We still love where we live, but have learned some lessons. If starting all over again, we would now seek a place not dominated by holiday homes. In our community there are 26 cottages, yet only 8 of those are permanently occupied. This results in a village which at some times in the year feels as if it lacks a soul. We have also suffered unpleasantness from a few insecure and aggressive residents who feel threatened by art and artists, bring more than our share of local discord, including with Argyll & Bute Council which is unsympathetic to small creative ventures and unable to assist them. One result has been the enforced removal of our sign from the nearby main road - hence our phoenixing into 'The Hidden Gallery' in response. But seek, and you shall find!

But we are in our community to stay, for as long as we can, and as long as it inspires us and motivates us. I am awed and stirred by the might of nature and that source of strength and beauty always close by in Argyll. My paintings are about raw, physical power and the passion and emotion it generates. A month ago Jean and I stood in a thunderstorm along the shore from our home, painting in the midst of the torrent and noise and thrilled to be able to do so.

I like to show the presence of the paint on the surface – warts and all! I work quickly on the spot catching the essence and the moment. I am not making a topographical copy – the digital camera, 'Photo Shop' and the wonders of giclee print can be used to do that, in their cold, soulless and repetitive way. The physical reality of the painting is a living thing.

In the *Arts Review,* September 1999, Marshall Anderson wrote: "McNeil's outdoor paintings bring about an emotional charge and expression of being Scottish through physical gesture. Within 45 minutes he wants to capture the moment, along with all its implications ..." I still want to do that, to feel and explore the 'emotional charge'. I always will: to me that charge is the essence of art. No matter what any one else thinks!

Don McNeil

Approaching Swan Nos 1 & 2

A Slash of Light – Gigha

The Silver Sail

A Slash of Light – Loch Fyne

The Rower No 1

Isle of May, Shrouded

The Heavens Opened

Sandstorm on Gigha

Portrait of a Crashing Wave

View from Kilchattan Bay

A Summer's Day

Colonsay from Mull

Loch Fyne Sunset over Furnace

Approaching Swan No 3

The Ghost Boat

Where Angels Tread

Alice Walsh

"I have a letter for Mr William Topaz McGonagall, Esquire." The young lad from the railway seemed pleased to have found me, the Poet McGonagall. Jeannie and I had but recently moved from Dundee, and it was no surprise to me that I was not known to all and sundry in the pleasant town of Perth. The boy was out of breath from climbing the stair and perspired heavily this fine October day. Jeannie gave him a drink of water while he waited for me to compose my reply.

The missive was an invitation from some gentlemen in Inverness to submit to their hospitality in return for an entertainment from me in the coming week. A sum of money for my trouble was mentioned, and all disbursements for my expenses would be generously found. I discussed this kind offer with Mistress McGonagall, she being wary of my public appearances of late, and we agreed that the money would be certain to come in useful, with the rent falling due on the first of the month. We were encouraged by the assurance of a hearty Highland welcome. I had not had occasion nor opportunity to visit those parts before and felt sure that the beauties of the town and its glorious surroundings would inspire my muse once more, subdued as it has been by recent events that occasioned our hasty departure from Dundee. Never will I set foot in that place again, though the City Fathers themselves get down on bended knees and beg me to return. I made haste to accept and prepared to be on my way.

The old gentleman in the dining room needed fed after his journey up from Perth. I prepared the repast myself; a piece of beef, some bread and coffee, as Mrs Macpherson was sleeping this hour. I took it through from the kitchen. I had minded not to burn the beef, or overscald the coffee, and made sure that the bread was from this morning's baking, not yesterday's, following Mr Macpherson's instructions. The gentleman, Mr McGonagall, did not look a wealthy or prosperous person, the sort that more usually demands Mr Macpherson's special attentions. His clothes were not too clean either, but he had the air of a body who knows that he is somebody, if you take my meaning. Mr Macpherson had told me he was a famous poet, though the way he laughed as he said it made me doubt he was truly sincere. In truth Mr McGonagall minded me of the Reverend Black in my old home near Fortrose. His spare frame, the deepset eyes that look straight through to your soul and his fey air of being in touch with otherworldly forces, were of that same stamp.

The gentleman thanked me most civilly for the vittles but declined the offer of wine with a vehemence that startled me.

"Drink is the work of the devil, child," he shouted, then perceiving my terror, lowered his voice and proceeded in a more gentle tone. "There's many a man whose reason is good enough when he is sober, but give him the drink and he will see his wife and bairns go cold and hungry in his lust for more." I could not but agree with him, having seen my father's brother's family descend to that very state before he was killed by his ox last winter. Jessie and the bairns bide with my father now, my mother being in her grave these past two years. The whole business was reason for me to leave home and find a living for myself here in Inverness.

"Sit down and keep me company while I eat." he bade me, so I took a seat for a minute or two, before seeing to the fires in the bedrooms. He asked my name. Upon my telling him it was Mary he began to sing;

> Oh charming Mary o' the Tay,
> Queen o' my soul by nicht and day.

and looked at me expectantly.

"Mr Macpherson said you are a famous poet," I ventured.

"Poet and tragedian," he nodded gravely. "I have given recitations to great gatherings in Scotland and all over the world," his face darkened some, "though they are a godless people in America and I was very glad to get back home. You will have heard of my most famous poem *The Railway Bridge of the Silvery Tay*, which inspired the Emperor of Brazil himself to come and view the bridge on his travels to Inverness." He saw from my face that I did not have the least idea of it and murmured gently, "Before your time, my dear, all before your time."

His face took on a look of such sadness that I became most anxious to lift his spirits. "And what will you be reciting tonight at the Banquet?" I enquired cheerfully.

He drew a deep breath. "First I'll give them *Bannockburn*, my own composition, perhaps you know it. No? I'll follow with a scene from *Macbeth*, which always stokes the fires in the belly, I find. And if they want some more, there's plenty more I can give them. I'll have to judge at the time what the gentlemen are in the humour for." He leaned towards me conspiratorially. "Sometimes they like to hear about a great tragedy, such as the sinking of the Storm Queen. Other times they have studied my works in depth and have their own favourites. I always bring copies of my most popular works. Perhaps you might like to study them?"

My duties did not allow me any further leisure that day nor much of the next as I explained to Mr McGonagall. I said that I was a good reader and would look for his work in the public library. I made my farewells and resumed my work about the hotel.

There was a fine turnout for the Banquet, must have been over fifty of the members and I'll wager we haven't seen some of them for ten years or more. "A splendid notion of yours, Gossip, to get McGonagall along," I told him. "By the Lord, I nearly pissed my breeches when he took so long to die … *Lay on MacDuff and damned be him that first cries 'Hold, enough'*" …

was it Macbeth he was playing?"

"Yes, Macpherson," Gossip replied breathing heavily, "but keep a hold of your tongue now awhile and take your share of the weight."

The two of us were escorting a rather drunken Poet back to his chambers after the most riotous evening I have enjoyed in a long while. Progress was slow as our charge would halt in his stumbles every few steps to recite another execrable couplet as he relived the triumph of his earlier rendition of *The Rattling Boy from Dublin*.

> *So with my darling shillelah, I gave him a whack,*
> *Which left him lying on his back,*
> *Saying, botheration to you and Biddy Brown,*
> *For I'm the rattling boy from Dublin Town.*
> *Whack fal de da, fal de darelido ...*

McGonagall's warblings were loud enough to rattle the beams of the hotel. He flailed his arms about wildly in his efforts to illustrate said whacking, resulting in what may well become a fine black eye for Gossip. All three of us were laid on the floor in a hopeless tangle. Then young Mary McFie came down the stairs to see what the rumpus was about. Bonny she was too, with her black hair in a long pleat and her face all flushed. She looked angry. I expect we disturbed her rest. Her appearance had a sobering influence, at least upon Gossip and me. To be fair, McGonagall did not know he had been drinking strong spirits, and was perhaps not as used to their effect. At any rate, when he set eyes on Mary, he began to weep. With some difficulty we got him to his feet. She took his arm and led him the few steps more to his room. Gossip and I thought it best to depart then and leave her to it.

I was sickened to the core when I saw what Mr Macpherson and Mr Gossip had done, doubtless with the connivance of those other feckless fellows in the Heather Blend Club. Always going too far, never caring who has to suffer for their high spirits or clean up after their jollifications. If I lose my position here, I won't care overmuch, though I'll not go back home, not ever. I manoeuvred Mr McGonagall as far as his bed without too much trouble but had to rush to fetch the basin for him, poor soul. I held it while he coughed up all he had inside him. He crumpled back onto the bed then, moaning quietly. I left water on his side table, removed his boots which were soiled with vomit, loosened his necktie and managed to push him over onto his side, in case the sickness should return. He neither hindered nor helped and all the while wore an expression on his face of a surprised bairn. He was asleep before I left the room.

I awoke the morning after the banquet with no very clear recollection of parts of the night before. I hoped that I had not suffered a *petit mal* as my father was wont to in his later years. I am nearing seventy years of age now, three score and ten is all that a man can reasonably hope for his stay upon God's green earth. I examined myself and found all my faculties were working, though I had a painful sensation about my head, and my stomach felt none too well. Hence I did not indulge too much at breakfast. The servant girl, Mary, served me with porridge and coffee. I thanked her for cleaning my boots so kindly, for they shone like polished jet upon my feet. For her kindness I gave her fair copies of some of my poems. I do believe there was a tear in her eye as she received them. It is a shame to deprive the servant classes of fine culture, when they so clearly relish the chance to dwell in its orbit. Mr Gossip, the kindly chairman of last evening's festivities, arrived to escort me to the railway station. He had injured himself about the eye in some grievous manner since I last saw him, but made little of any discomfort and offered no explanation. Mary's face, as I bade her farewell wore a look of such sweet sorrow that I was inspired to write a few lines on the journey home.

> The Banquet was held in the Gellion Hotel
> And the landlord Mr Macpherson, treated me right well
> Also the servant maids were very kind to me,
> Especially the girl who polished my boots most beautiful to see.

In truth, I felt it was Mary, rather than the boots, who was most beautiful to see. I recalled a dream I'd had the night before of a ministering angel who bore a strong resemblance to the girl. I felt it best to leave my admiration a wee bit hidden in the poem, which will surely become well known, as I don't want my Jeannie to have any cause for jealousy. That's the best way to keep the mistress happy as I have found over the years.

Owen Gallagher

Bagpipes

I want to be that lone bagpipe player,
in the field, in full dress, under the motorway,
pumping up the sun on this icy morning,
forcing leaves out on trees,
a forgotten clan out of a glen,
and the monster from Loch Ness.
I want to play at the opening of all Highland Games,
from Braemar to the Cowal Gathering,
and pipe off a triumphant Scottish football team
at the next World Cup Games.

The drone of the pipes reminds me of their banning,
clearances, heroes, kilts and dirks,
forcing me to abandon my jog along the canal.
I feel like a celebrity
as I am piped into this London field,
by this magical, mantelpiece figure,
in a Munro, MacLean, or MacPharlan tartan,
who could tease salmon from the river
and wandering Scots abroad back home.

The cars above him halt, windows lowered,
engines silenced, drivers and passengers lured out
by this piper in the field, on the eve
of when we must address the haggis.

Miss Jennings' Departure

I recommend her without reservation,
an excellent lover, composer,
player of the skin, a collaborator
who can move from a sonata
to a full orchestra piece without a script,

the skin – a blank stave for her to play,
all minims, semi-breves, quavers,
each bodily part singled out for a recital,
to bow and withdraw,
letting the whole movement perform solo,

until conductor and participant
lie exhausted, entwined,

a double clef, paused,
eager to commence a new score.

Already I feel the absence
of her signature tune.

Backyards

They sit in their back garden, in raincoats,
deckchairs, in the heat of summer,
sharing a poke of chips,
they pretend they are at the seaside,
kiss the salt off each other's fingers, lips,
point to something out at sea, giggle,
chattering loud as seagulls.

Their hearing aids must be off. Hands glide
like wings, couple in mid-air.
She screams at the tide lapping their feet.
and hauls him to the island
that is their home. I catch a glimpse of clothes
being shed, nakedness. They disappear
to dry out from the heat in each others skin.

My love is in her wheelchair, I wipe her chin.
I'm reminded of a boat, a moon,
an orchestra on our honeymoon.
I ask her to dance, hoist her into the air.
We waltz through Marseilles, Rome,
and Capri, until musicians tire. Make our way
beneath the sea, swim in each others arms.

At the Rattle of the Rosaries

When she knelt, the whole house knelt,
the sky would open
and we'd be catapulted from earth,
glad to be away, safe in a place of our own
as if in a belly, suspended by a cord of prayer,
anchored to a world where we suffocated
until evening prayers.
Then mother would click, click,
her fingers and we'd land with a thud,
plucking feathers from our arms,
hanging wings the size of swans
behind the door.

Andrew R C Hamilton

In the Beginning

May I tell you my story? Of necessity it will be short for I have lived for only 15 months. Most of that period has been delightful.

For months I lay around in the warmth and comfort of my mother's womb. It maybe more accurate to say I swam around but as I never took any lessons I made little or no progress.

Occasionally, my mother and I, inseparable at that time, would go along to the doctor's clinic where he would place a stethoscope on my mummy's tummy and listen to my heart beat. He seemed anxious about me but he need not have worried for I was as strong as could be and was enjoying the environment in which I was developing. Then he would take pictures of me, which he displayed on a screen and discussed with my mother. They commented on how strong I was and how handsome I would be. It was then I learned I would be photogenic and I intend to exploit that later. My mother was so happy and so proud of me. She would burst into tears of joy as soon as we were back in the privacy of our house.

What worried me was that I was sure there was a great big world out there from which I was temporarily excluded. I yearned for the day Mother Nature would decide that I had better forego the feather-bedded life I was enjoying and go out to face whatever was in store for me.

One thing that annoyed me (for early in life I became a critic) was that I was not able to determine exactly when I should leave the protection, comfort and cosiness of my mother's womb. I thought long and hard on this and decided that I had found the first situation over which I did not have personal control. This was a salutary lesson I have remembered for the rest of my short life. You may wonder why I am conversant with so much technical data, but that is easily explained. Daily I listened to conjecture centred around my existence and occasionally listened to technicians explaining to students just how I was evolving. I heard so much of this that at the end of this term of my life I could have sat an examination on midwifery and child development.

There was, of course, one bridge to cross: the transition from the womb to outer space. I had given this some thought and decided I would come out head-first. That was a good decision for, as I learned later, any other approach was fraught with danger.

My mum did not enjoy the experience as much as I had hoped she would. She was often in tears as she drew in her breath while trying to force me from her. She should have known I would be reluctant to leave her. I could not understand the hurry. When there was talk of opening her up to lift me from her, unceremoniously, I knew the time had come for me to capitulate and go through the process of being born. As soon as I co-operated the difficulties being experienced by my mother disappeared and I found myself being hauled into a new world. The change from the womb to the reality of independent existence was so great I registered my disapproval immediately. I had heard that unless one did so one received a smack on ones bottom and I did not want this show of force to be my introduction into the world.

My yelling was greeted with smiles and sighs of approval, even of relief, so that the very first thing I had done was the correct thing to do. I was mighty pleased with myself. On reflection, I could not understand why these adults were so pleased with me because, since then, when I yell I am counselled to shut up. From this experience I learned how two faced humans are, how inconsistent and how difficult to understand. That being so, I was a wee bit disappointed that I was born a human being. I think I was really meant to be an angel.

As soon as I sucked in my first breath of fresh air, I was wrapped up like a Christmas present and placed in my mother's arms. Instead of being pleased she wallowed in tears. Admittedly, I am an ugly little animal but, I am assured, lovely in her eyes. She had been overcome by what she considered my beauty. She counted the number of fingers on both hands and the number of toes. I knew she should be using the Dewy Decimal system but, regrettably, she never had that level of education. It should not be surprising that I understand such matters for my doing so is nothing compared with the miracle of my birth which everyone takes for granted.

She also examined every other aspect of my body and decided I was normal. Just as well she could not see beneath the skin or she may have been more than worried for I know I am going to be a little devil.

In the months since then I have drank milk from my mother's breast, eaten soft solids, wet the bed and tried hard to understand what is going on around me. Presumably, I have made errors of deduction. Regrettably, I cannot communicate this problem with any of the many fuddy-duddies who come to see me for I cannot make the sort of sounds which they use with one another. I can only belch, fart, yell, scream and cry. When my mummy talks to me I understand what she is saying and I would dearly love to be able to talk back to her but when I open my mouth unintelligible sounds emerge, strange even to my immature ears. I have decided that the most urgent job I must tackle is to learn this technique of communication. How I will do so is not understood. It is, in fact, a mystery but if I try hard glimmers of light will fill my darkness.

For weeks after I was born I lay on my back, slept when I felt like sleeping and roared when I needed food. My every wish was attended to. I found it difficult to believe that life would continue to be like this, and how true that was. Now although I am but a few months old I am constantly harassed. My life is not my own. I have to lie down, sit up, eat, or sleep, or smile for my aunties, or look interested in other babies who are supposed to be like me but could not hold a candle to me. I am slave to my mummy's fancies. I know she tries to be so good to me and, in return, I wish to be kind to her, but she does strain my patience at times.

When I have learned how to talk to her I will keep her right. When she recognises she has a child prodigy on her hands she will be flummoxed, not knowing how to cope with me. But I will coo to her, smile my widest smile and tell her not to worry for I will grow up to be a credit to her.

Now that I have a few words I keep asking her: "Where is my father?" She says that is a silly question for today we don't need fathers any more. That being so I hope I am a baby girl for baby boys, I am told, grow up to be fathers. And I have a fear of redundancy.

A Shaggy Dog Story

I hope you enjoy reading this very short story. If you do not please do not blame me. For I disclaim responsibility. There is a pen in my hand and I am making marks on paper. But it is not me who is directing the pen.

Rightly you ask: "Who, then, is it who is moving the pen across the paper?" and I must reply that I am not at all too sure. My suspicion is that it is my lovely pet dog, put down some 14 days ago, who is the real writer of this tale. I am sure it is he for, yesterday evening I heard him bark, unmistakably his bark, the one he uses to tell me he wants something. That used to be food, but he no longer requires material sustenance.

I am confused! What could he want? When I had thought about this for some time I realised he wanted me to get off this sofa on which I was dozing, and get across to my desk, something he had seen me do a thousand times. I must have guessed correctly for as soon as I sat down at my desk his barking stopped. Normally this is what I do when some idea comes in to my mind and I feel I must get it down on paper lest I lose it forever. But there is nothing on, or in, my mind so why am I sitting here?

I have now sat here for what seems an interminable time, pen in hand, paper before me, but nothing comes into my mind, nothing I would commit to paper. Now his barking has resumed and I know he wants me to write something down for him, something which he wants me to know. I feel I have no alternative but to do as he wishes. And this is what I, or was it he, wrote:

"Margaret, this is Sphinx back again to annoy you. I want you to do something for me. The lovely, succulent bone you gave me a few days before I left you, but could not eat because I felt terrible and my appetite was gone, I have hidden beneath the kitchen sink. Would you take it out and give it to my wee pal Sally next door who will love that delicacy.

Also, I have a surprise for you. You will recall taking me to the vet to have 'the business' done. He asked you to leave me as he was so busy that day. Well, he did not do as you asked. There were too many dogs to be seen that day and he got thoroughly mixed up so that although he deceived you by charging for an operation he did not do, do not be too hard on him, for I have enjoyed life far more than I would have done otherwise.

And, you should have guessed, Sally is one of mine, my daughter, I am pleased to say. I could have selected a better mother for her but she was the only one available that day. And that bonny, mixed breed spaniel who lives at the end of the street, she's mine as well. To be frank, almost every dog in the vicinity has a wee bit of me in him. What a fine bunch they are!

You must have wondered why at times I barked so loudly. Now you know. I could feel the spirit of the chase coming over me and wanted out to do my duty by my fellow dogs, ensuring the continuation of the doggy breeds.

When you walk down the village I will no longer be with you, or so it would seem, but every time you come to my progeny I will cough a little, just to let you know I'm here beside you, and that the dog you are passing owes its presence to my activity. I must say I had a good life under your tutelage, but I am not sure who I should thank, you or that silly big vet.

Good-bye – Sphinx."

Jim C Wilson

Three Tanka Concerning Loss

On this grey March day
wondering about a cup
of coffee and you
I notice the place we met
is boarded up and for sale.

Before the mists clear
I am at your locked front door
holding half a poem.
As I wait, it's spring again.
Again the blossom, the words.

This year the berries
on the holly tree appear
more red than ever.
So many – so many months
since opening your last letter.

Thirteen Lines

As I stretch to pluck the imperfect fruit
I see the prints of your fingers and lips
but, whoever you are, our poem's incomplete.

I listen for breathing that is not mine,
remembering how a kiss needed courage,
how love came and went like the sea.

(You said we must not upset applecarts.
So there was no music in the wind.)

Aware of the stinging, the newest drops of blood,
I just don't know, don't know how it will end.

Autumn is back with its dead leaves circling.
The sudden white moth flies so close,
and images crack like dull broken moons.

Their Garden

Late autumn, yet the stream is just a trickle.
A mass of crows is watching from the oak
while, muffled in old clothes, he tidies leaves.
She's inside, reading, thinking of abroad –
and how the airport's now impossible.
Funny how the hours and years get shorter

and yet that sky grows bigger every day.
They'd planned to change the place, adapt, convert,
but now the bathroom window glass stays cracked.
The evergreen they planted years go
had seemed a kind of symbol of their love.
One winter it had withered, nearly died.
A subject for a poem, perhaps, he thinks,
as weakening sunlight filters through the branches,
disappears, and leaves him wondering in the shade.

Adelaide at Saranac *

With time to kill and winter near,
she created a new form of verse:
twenty-two syllables, five short lines.
Ideal to pass her hours away.

No point in starting something big;
one image really says it all.
Like the sudden white moth that flew
so close as the short day darkened,

grew so cold. She sat on the porch
counting the weeks – and syllables:
two, then four, then six, then eight. Two
brought the brief surprising end.

Sunk in her robe, she wrote cinquains,
heard passing ghosts in brittle leaves.
Was she convinced that little was more,
there, with that spondee, slow TB?

* *The American poet, Adelaide Crapsey, invented the cinquain form. She died in 1914, aged 36.*

Two Cinquains
Untreated

Lichen
creeps green across
the leaning fence and takes
each board, slow, into the waiting
landscape.

Unkindest

My spade
descends and cuts
the earth and now the worm
that singularly slid through slime
is two.

Mr Iain and Mr Iain (M) … (Banks)

Edmund O'Connor

H G Wells is a good place to begin to consider Iain Banks. One is a giant of English literature and father of science fiction; the other an *enfant explosif*. But Wells is the author of 'scientific romances' – and a keen social critic: in *Kipps* and *Mr Lewisham Takes a Holiday* the former drapers' assistant kicks out at a class system that condemns people to wage-slavery. His social concerns fed into his fantastical writing: *The Time Machine* is critical of how humanity toils, debasing itself into oblivion, or idles and beautifies itself into nothingness. He makes no distinction between the two sides of his writing – neither to be praised above the other. Banks's work has not been so fortunate. While his mainstream work *has* been looked at with some seriousness, critical attention passes over his science fiction – the strange case of Mr Iain Banks and Mr Iain M Banks.

"A work of unparalleled depravity", "a repulsive piece of work", "a gloatingly sadistic and grisly yarn", – so the literary world greeted *The Wasp Factory*. Published in 1984, three years after the sweeping surrealism of Alasdair Gray's *Lanark*, it was everything a novel shouldn't be: short (184 pages), and nasty (the 'hero', Frank, multiple murderer at 16, gleefully tortures animals). Surely he and his nasty book would soon crawl back into the Scottish slime. Twenty-three books and two decades and a place on the 1993 *Granta* Young Writers List later, London has warmed to the boy from the north. His last 'proper' novel (*Dead Air*) was even set there, with past books *Walking on Glass* and *Whit* featuring the metropolis in strong walk-on parts. From the north itself though, silence.

In issue 1, *Scottish Review of Books*, Rosemary Goring ruffles a few feathers of Scottish literary pride. We *have* world-class talents, (Kelman, Galloway and Gray); most of the rest is good, but not world-beating. While Ian Rankin out-grimes everyone else, and Alexander McCall Smith tickles ladies' fancies, these mega-sellers don't represent the best Scottish writing. Kelman, Galloway and Welsh produce the true classics, the "snow-tipped Himalayas amid a sea of Lammermuirs". Fair enough.

One name omitted was that of Banks, not even raised to be swept aside? Goring declares: "Scottish writers … are frequently ignored by English literary pages. The heart of the British literary establishment still beats in London." Many Scottish writers who *are* noticed by the literary establishment "live in the English literary heartland", diluting the "off-putting scent of clannishness". Banks is interviewed by *The Guardian* and others, and while reviews of his book, *Raw Spirit*, were a little below spontaneous praise, it was a brave editor who ignored it. There still seems to linger a suspicion that Banks doesn't write, he just types with style. Why?

"The most imaginative British novelist of his generation", said *The*

Times of Banks. *City Limits* of Banks's *Lanark* homage, *The Bridge*: "[it contains] references to the kinds of reality that rarely gets into British literature". Fay Weldon: "The great white hope of contemporary British literature". If *Granta* had claimed him for London, London can keep him. The old Scots tendency of knocking success is alive and kicking. And if knocking doesn't work, ignoring it is just as useful. He be not 'merely' a Scottish writer, but a 'British' one, thus excluded from serious debate. It's clear that while Banks himself may have reservations about whether he *is* a Scottish novelist, some of his roots *are* in the Scottish tradition.

Scots didn't invent the idea of antisyzygy, but have become good at deploying it. But both *Shattered Glass* and *The Bridge* deploy not just two, but three disparate strands, *Shattered Glass* being the most potent example. The very title suggests a broken whole, a mirror to see ourselves in. Graham Park, an amiable, if unlucky art student in love, Steven Grout, a man consumed by paranoia with a tenuous grasp on reality, and Quiss, a warrior condemned to play outlandish games in a purgatory composed entirely of books, don't have much in common, but they all come together in the end. Park walks through Grout's story, which also part of Quiss's. The parts only make sense when seen in the whole: hence the mistake in seeing the book as *three* stories, rather than *one* with three levels.

But while *Walking on Glass* is a perfectly serious book, it is on another level not serious at all. It is not a post-modern novel, but rather 'post-post-modern' – taking the rise out of the concept for being too clever for its own good. Banks is surely stretching credulity with six 'parts' in less than 240 pages, making each part a mere 'sliver' (yet another joke – a gentle ribbing of his hero Gray's use of mixed-up books in *Lanark).*

Near the end, Ajayi, Quiss's fellow inmate, picks out one book in their castle prison, and starts to read: "He walked through the white corridors ..." The book she's starting is the one the reader is finishing: the ultimate self-reference, so there is both a 'joke', and the reader can see 'beyond' the book's 'end' to a point where the novel is the reason for its own extension. The novel has the archness and occasional bouts of smugness of the concept it's trying to undercut – but is also a valuable aid to realising why Banks is excluded from modern critical debate. There are no sacred cows in his universe: just different parts of consciousness, seen only through different eyes and styles, hence his toying with realism, pseudo-realism and quasi-science-fiction in the same book. Or thrillers in *Canal Dreams.* Or the rock memoir in *Espedair Street.* Or the family saga in *The Crow Road.*

Banks doesn't play the self-conscious game of being a Scottish Writer, often setting books outwith Scotland, without Scottish characters or use of Scots. The one time he does, in *The Bridge*, is for the meat-headed barbarian, a parody of a typical male Scot. This could be seen as taking the piss out of the language rather than the stereotype, but he associates himself much less with Scotland than other writers and is more a writer who happens to be Scottish, rather than a Scot who happens to write.

Banks's writing challenges both 'Scottish writing' – and 'novel writing' itself. The 'postmodern novel' may have overtaken the 'Hampstead' as *the* way to write, but their after-effects are keenly felt today. 'Proper' novels favour interior dialogue over exterior action and contain complicated ideas you only 'get' after having 'absorbed' the book. They are *not* supposed to be written quickly, to feature physical action as mental as *The Crow Road*'s exploding granny, and be great fun to read. And successful too. But Banks does all these: so his books aren't seen as 'real work'. They challenge too many preconceived ideas about what a novel 'should' be.

Banks spends 8-9 months doing what he likes best: visiting sci-fi conventions, seeing his pals, arseing about in boats or bombing around in his prized BMW M5. About September, he gets down to the next novel, not raising his head until mid-December. Proofs are sent in January, leaving him again to live the life of Riley. *Dead Air,* in fact, probably set no records at all for being completed in just six weeks. (MacDiarmid, legendarily, wrote *Lucky Poet* (400 pages) in a week.) Banks himself pre-empted the criticism: "Obviously that it means it was dashed off in a moment of nonsense and can't be a real book". Garrets, garrets, garrets.

The sheer action that Banks packs into his work might make us think this is just 'cinema with words', all action and no reflection. But behind all the action, killing, explosions, is observation and analysis. *The Crow Road*, for instance, does feature the infamous combusting grandmother, but *is* about big issues: death, family, religion and the nature of truth … Prentice McHoan, charged with discovering why Uncle Rory disappeared, finds he's swimming in treacherous waters: Fergus, his pompous, Thatcherite uncle-in-law, becomes an infinitely darker character thanks to Prentice's discoveries. Though enraged by his wife's infidelity, Fergus only murders when no-one realises he has anything to do with it. Since Fergus drunkenly told Rory the sordid story, Fergus feels he has no option but to kill his brother-in-law too to keep the secret. So they both die: Rory, for keeping silent; and Fergus for murdering his wife.

Religion also figures strongly, with the McHoan brothers all taking a different spiritual path. Kenneth, Prentice's father, is an out-and-out communist; Uncle Hamish commits the ultimate Protestant act by breaking off and forming his own peculiar Christian sect; while Rory's religion (or lack thereof) is less dogmatic and more mysterious. Prentice goes on a spiritual journey of his own, from unquestioning acceptance of his father's version, to outright rejection of it. Although there are the requisite 'sitting round the table earnestly debating religion' moments, Banks shows resonances beyond the chin-stroking.

Kenneth and Hamish, wandering home both worse the wear for booze, break a cardinal rule of drinking: never talk religion. As Hamish tells it: "he [Kenneth] said; 'Hamish; all the gods are false. Faith itself is idolatry"'. As they near Shore Street Church, Kenneth decides to prove his brother wrong by climbing the church tower. But an outside hand intervenes: lightning strikes the tower, electrocuting Kenneth. Hamish, though distraught, is emphatic as a Presbyterian minister: Kenneth is spitting in God's eye: "Jealous, Prentice; jealous! Jealous! Jealous God! Jealous!" Banks doesn't have much time for Christianity (being more sympathetic to communism), but the lightning episode points out what stupid things unquestioning faith in any form compels people to do.

The idea of the postmodern and Hampstead novel has been applied far beyond its context. The latter is nice people doing nice things, the post-modern novel is nasty people doing even worse things, while Banks's work is imperfect people doing often misjudged things. He just doesn't get a reputation because his writing's not fashionable. *Lanark* was a smash hit because it hit the market during a coincidental flourishing of postmodernism in the south, and was therefore fashionable.

But fashion dictates that he remains *persona non grata* in the metropolis. He's too 'full-on' for them, and has little time for the work still being praised there. "The Hampstead novel – zzz – sound of author going to sleep. There doesn't seem to be a lot of stuff around that makes sense". And: "I've nothing against Hampstead novels, as such. But I do have a problem with them being held up as the most important or respectable genre ... Elevating it almost becomes a sort of bigotry, saying that science fiction must be worse, less important." (*Interzone*, 1986)

Arthur C Clarke apart, it's difficult to think of a more popular living 'British' science fiction author than Iain M Banks. But why has this side of his work been ignored by the mainstream press. The sad fact is that science fiction has been a dead area critically for some time now, the giant imaginations of Clarke, Isaac Asimov, Dick, etc sidelined by the main-stream, left to specialist magazines like *Interzone*, *SFX* & co to pick over.

From Wells' *War of the Worlds*, through Fritz Lang's *Metropolis*, the *Flash Gordon* serials, to *2001: A Space Odyssey*, *Dune*, *Do Androids Dream of Electric Sheep?*, SF has many modes: serious, funny, sad, epic, intimate, social commentary ... Banks is tapping into the most amazing flights of fancy, where imagination is freed of the shackles of 'reality'. But critics see science fiction as a denial of reality, an inability to live in the world which surrounds us. But reality often blinds us to essential truths, and those layers need to be stripped away, in part or entire, to see these truths.

The problem is literature's refusal to discuss, let alone acknowledge the serious things SF is saying, including in Scotland, though David Linday's *Voyage to Arcturus* enjoyed a brief spell of popularity in the 80s. Far from running away from real-world concerns, the best SF uses the fantastic and science as a basis for examining ourselves from other angles, not as a slave of science. *Jekyll and Hyde* uses science to ponder that ultimate question: who are we? Brian McHale points out: "post-

Iain Banks (photograph © John Foley)

modernism and science fiction can be seen as siblings, sharing a common descent in the 20th century ... these sister genres [go] along parallel but independent tracks". *SRB* reader Stuart Allcroft, responsed to Banks's absence in Goring's article: "Some genres are obviously more equal than others"! As Banks says: "all science fiction stories are still about recognisable human beings ... unless there's some kind of emotional dimension or plot dynamic that makes sense to the human emotions, it's going to be impossible to read the damn things with any degree of pleasure".

Banks's main focus is on a galactic scale: a vast, technologically-obsessed, semi-communist civilisation, the Culture. In the early pages of *Consider Phlebas* there are vast space fleets, spaceships with Minds of their own and a galaxy-spanning conflict between the Culture and the Idrians (who worship religion as fervently as the Culture do technology). Big ships, big guns and even bigger plots – an almost child-like glee fills the writing compared to his relatively pedestrian 'mainstream' works. As Banks himself has said: "There may well be more art in the miniature, but by God, it's more fun in the bigger visions". No wonder he calls his SF works 'space operas' – epics that "out-*Star-Wars Star Wars*". As Brian W Aldiss said of Alfred Bester's work– it's "Wide-Screen Baroque, a free-wheeling interplanetary adventure, full of brilliant scenery, dramatic scenes and a joyous taking for-granted of the unlikely".

So SF writing is a harmless hobby. Even *The Independent*'s admiring review of *Look to Windward* saw his SF writing as a "sub-career". Even *Interzone* was surprised about his 'new' direction: "What's all this nonsense about wanting to write science fiction?" But he'd already written five novels, three SF, before his debut was published. His first foray into SF, *Consider Phlebas*, was finished by the time *The Wasp Factory* came out.

Complicity, a 'mainstream' work, deploys an (un)divine retribution against those who profit by Thatcherism: the first victim dies by an iron railing through the head, and the rest fare not much better: judges, porn barons, all fall to the killer's blade. As the killer in *Complicity* comments: "There wasn't one of those men who hadn't killed people; indirectly, the way the Nuremberg Nazis did", expressing Banks's overpowering rage at those who cynically destroy a way of life. Andrew Gimson, who dismissed *The Wasp Factory* as "soaring to the level of mediocrity" in *The Times*, worked in: "Conservative Party Central Office. So I went 'Yeahhh!' I didn't want a good review from those bastards. It was just priceless".

Even using 'M' in his name to differentiate his work (a backwards homage to Aldiss, who wrote SF with the W dropped) has played into the hands of his critics. In a 1996 interview to *Wired*, he commented: "I regret doing it, intensely now ... it passes on ammunition to the literary snobs who just assume that I make the distinction because I'm writing down when I'm writing science fiction". Banks just cannae win.

Banks says: "Nothing and nobody in the Culture is exploited". In

Consider Phlebas and in subsequent books, his trick is to set the novels *around* the Culture, but rarely actually *in* it. From the start of *Consider Phlebas* Banks teases the reader: the 'hero' is technically one of the bad guys, we see an independent 'orbital' destroyed by the Culture. We go on a former Culture vessel, but only get the tiniest glimpses of the Culture itself. Banks is inviting debate on the nature of society – is the Culture reaching paradise, or a bunch of clueless hedonists who have traded their minds for technology? Does letting technology run your life destroy your soul? Banks clearly thinks not, but we need to hear the argument.

Banks's point is that technology, far from enslaving humanity, can help free us to create the nearest thing to Utopia: "[it's] the use of technology to create a social space in which exploitation and oppression can't exist". This is a specific response to right-wing high-octane epics like *Starship Troopers* where humanity is at the service of machines to construct neo-imperialist empires. The set-up is run by the 'Minds', vast artificial intelligences who can outwit most people under the Culture's benevolent umbrella. But it's not a story of humanity being superfluous in its own design – there are a select band who can outguess even the combined might of massed Minds: a 'Culture Referrer', such as Fal 'Ngeestra in *Consider Phlebas*, is highly prized. For all Banks's gentle needling of the Culture's absurdities – the backbone of the Culture war-fleet is the deadly General Contact Vehicles – he's deeply in love with the ethos behind it.

Critics of Banks, in SF mode, are can't look past the bonkers names for spaceships such as *No More Mr Nice Guy*, *I Blame the Parents* and the barely pronounceable ones (Juboal-Rabaroansa Perosteck Alseya Balveda dam T'seif, anyone?) and see the meat beneath the tomfoolery. Banks has short shrift for this: "The genre bloody well ought to be out of short trousers by now". The SF authors who write to their own audience's expectations by producing what has memorably been termed 'fanwank' are at least part of the problem of getting a general audience to take the genre seriously.

Too Scottish for London, not Scottish enough for Scotland, too violent by half and too obsessed by SF for his own good – these are some things which stop Banks and his work from being taken seriously. Although the Association of Scottish Literary Studies has made a start with its Scotnotes on *The Wasp Factory*, *The Crow Road* and *Whit* there is much more to be done, especially with his science fiction. We will never get to grips with Banks as long as we overlook half his output, just as we can't look at Wells by viewing his 'scientific romances' only. Penguin has taken the long-overdue step of releasing 10 of Wells's best in its 'Classics' series. Will we have to wait until 2106 before something similar happens to Banks, and his writing is viewed in the round, not in the half? But it's not as if he cares, really. His books are written to entertain himself, and if anyone else is entertained, that's fine. If not, so be it. The snobs can go stuff themselves while he has a whale of a time.

Ultrameta

Douglas Thompson

When I walk out into this city, the sky swallows me. Always at dusk and in autumn, I wake up when everyone else has finished their day's tribulations. I begin again, like the butterfly from its cocoon, reborn briefly, to choose another name, another death. The sky is blue turning black, and the clouds tinged with colour seem to rush towards me, or to wherever I fix my eyes on the hemisphere above, as if to mop my brow. Each day destroys me in the end, uses me up, because I open myself to it so utterly.

The clothes don't matter. They don't even smell of me, in so far as I even remember who I'm supposed to be. Ideally, they are somebody else's, borrowed or stolen, and if they just hang there on me, so much the better. I walk, let's say in a suit I don't even recognise, and it feels strange and loose against my skin. That's comforting because it means I don't know it and it doesn't know me – that's fresh because then anything can happen. I'm wiped clean every time, memory and identity gone, a mystery and a stranger to myself and to all the other strangers I pass. This is freedom.

I choose any direction then walk under the darkening sky, collar turned up, in this city I call *Ultrameta* because nothing stands still here. I look for clues: the grain of sand in the oyster's shell, the smallest fragment can start me off in this evening's journey to invent an identity. A traffic light changes to green, a falling leaf in a park turning in mid-flight can point to a street where a light suddenly goes on or off in an intriguing way that makes me want to make my life go there. Then I just go. No baggage that I remember, I can take these choices lightly. No job, wife, children, parents, passport, driving licence, bank card, no anchor – so I drift forever.

I walk into an anonymous coffee-bar, where specimens of the evening's flotsam like me sit perched at the counter on stools, crows on telephone wires. The light is too harsh and there are mirrors in unexpected places, so I can glimpse myself, who I might be and whoever might be watching me. These are my real clues: until somebody speaks to me I am nobody, I have no personality. But a few words are all I need, a look in the eyes and soon I can tell them what they want to hear and construct myself to suit.

A girl with brown eyes comes in and starts talking to me; her hair is long and straight. I can see her back reflected in that mirror. Suddenly she is talking urgently into my face, telling me she thinks she knows me. I look so like the husband of a friend she was talking to last week, and she can't understand why I don't recognise her. I can see her mouth but the sound somehow doesn't reach me. My eyes roll until I'm watching the surface of the coffee sitting on the glass counter top closely from the corner of my eye. I'm seeing it closer and larger until it fills my field of vision. There are waves crashing across it with crests of foam, and a vortex is turning there like a typhoon. I grab her mouth, lean closer and look into her eyes. Then

I see everything that's there all in an instant: her entire life from start to finish, what will happen next and how it will end.

It's all so quiet again: she's stopped talking. I move my head to one side to glimpse myself in the mirror. I see ears, see my hair and chin, but in the centre there's only a hole with cogs turning inside: ancient, blackened cogs, some fast, some slow, but all of them unstoppable. I grab her shoulders and spin her around on her seat to see this reflection and as she turns my face appears over the cogs, sliding from left to right just as her eyes pass over it. And I'm complete again for now, I have an identity.

I lean down and kiss her left cheek, then look at our reflection again. I pay for us, and we walk out into the labyrinth. The city is white in the moonlight now, like bones. We walk, the jagged shards jut up against the sky. The whole city is a skeleton and we're walking through its rib cage. My companion is taking my hand, leading me to the top of a hill where we wait for traffic lights to change as a flow of ghostly white cars whistle through, shimmering with speed. There is a noise of tarmac and stone cracking. Buildings slide past in front of us, dust and debris billowing out from under their ragged bases. An entire city block, like stage scenery on the move, is changing location to seven blocks downhill – a more desirable area. The group huddle together, their roofs and towers, steeples and flags sticking up like the heraldry of a bold nocturnal crusade. In some passing windows I can see perfectly normal domestic scenes: clothing being ironed, dinner served for a family of four. The dust settles and the lights change again. We cross the road before buses advance on us.

She's leading me somewhere. Towards the moon, where it hovers low over the ocean. Walking downhill again, I notice the tall buildings thinning out as we approach a more derelict area. Old buildings have collapsed or been demolished: whole blocks have been cleared away and only the pavements are left, with solitary lamp-posts hanging over us, flickering in a state of disrepair. She's calmed down now as we walk, punches my arm playfully and says: *So do you remember me now? Or are you not who I say you are? Why have you changed your appearance?*

I don't know who I am, I answer her truthfully. *Nor you either. Does it matter? What or who am I supposed to be? What kind of man is the one I look like? Should I apologise for him? I don't mind apologising for him, since I have none of his pride, presuming he has any. But defending him … will be more difficult, without some more knowledge.*

Madman, she says, looking at me with a mock-deranged expression, *I can't figure you out. You're either a madman or you're addicted to melodrama … to romance at any cost. Or then again … maybe you ARE somebody else?*

I feel like I AM somebody else, this time I think … on balance. This time? *Yes – I feel there have been many times, is that not the case?*

I don't know, she says, her voice dropping, *… not this bad …*

At last we come to a solitary house, surreal because everything around it has been removed, a grand little town house with overgrown garden and rusting Victorian gates. I run my hands round its fantastical twists and volutes. A tram rattles by behind us, shaking the ground as we walk across the moonlit garden; The surface of a bright pond ripples, silver against the black hues of the ivy twisting everywhere across the ground.

Inside she leads me in semi-darkness up a broad staircase into an upper room with a bare wooden floor; its planks creak under our feet. The walls, the ornate cornice and skirtings, are all painted black, but I can dimly make out white lines; astronomical diagrams and geometry theorems, like intellectual graffiti. *I would have liked you to meet my father,* she says shyly. She gestures to where he stands at the window, looking out over the view of the great bone-hard city on the hill, the derelict plain beneath it, and the dark ocean off to the right. The window is large, full-height like patio doors, but old and sub-divided into many panes by peeling mullions and astragals. The rough sackcloth curtains are fawn and laden with dust. Stepping closer, I see that her father is actually a white plaster bust, a heroic Edwardian torso with a chequered waistcoat buttoned round him, perched on the chipped plastic legs of a tailor's dummy. But his head turns, his deathly-white features flex a little and he speaks in a weary, hushed tone: *Ahh! You've come again I see, I expected as much. Will she remember anything this time?*

But father, I say, *I've never seen her before in my life, though conceivably in my dreams, if I'm not dreaming now. And anyway, how do you know me?*

Fool, he says. *Nobody knows you. Except maybe the inanimate like me and innocent children like her, before you close her eyes forever. Why do you torment us by coming here? Isn't it enough that the city fathers demolish our district stone by stone, year after year to prepare for the next stage of their great plan: to make new glass palaces for the heartless ones, the maestros of youth and savagery?*

I feel a hand on my left arm. His daughter has come to rescue me. I look at her soft living face and smile, then back to her father who is now just a lifeless statue again, grey and inert, but with a single droplet of moisture on his cheek which I reach out and catch with my finger. I hold it out to her, but a cloud of the turbulent night sky clears, the beams of moonlight intensify, falling across the empty floor of the living room. As we watch, the floor changes into a silvery ocean, criss-crossed by tiny waves. Enchanted, we link hands and walk slowly across it towards the black rectangle of the open hall door, the moonlit water lapping over our toes.

She takes me up a further staircase of creaking timber, narrower this time, into a large attic with skylights propped open to the night air. The room has been a library, and I see shelves around the room but notice that most of the books are heaped in a pile in the middle of the floor. She grows quiet and walks in front, reverently, kneels at the base of the pile and begins picking up one book after the other to examine it.

I walk slowly closer. She picks up each ancient book, wipes its cover clear of dust, reads the title, opening the first few pages, skimming gradually through the rest then sighs and discards the book onto the pile. Then she picks up the next one, on and on, *ad infinitum*. The process becomes frantic, her hands darting in agitation. I kneel down next to her; her eyes are filled with tears. I put both my hands over hers and close them over the book she holds. Her body stills and calms at last, its unexplained disturbance fading away. I pick up a few books myself, fill my arms with a bundle and take them over to an open skylight. She follows me. Our eyes meet, agreeing a sort of plan. Standing by the window, we take each book one by one, then piles at a time, and hurl them up into the starry night sky. Most just open up into the air, white pages fluttering, then fall off to the left, caught by the wind, and bounce away, thumping off the roof slates as they fall to the ground. But our eyes light up and we laugh exultantly at this: every tenth book or so hovers longer, flutters its white pages, then lifts off and flaps away into the night, flying towards the ocean and freedom. We laugh and shout as we continue, freeing and condemning books at random for over an hour, until the attic is empty.

At last we are left without a single book, staring at each other, the old sadness returning. The night wind blows across our faces in the silence, the same wind with its smells of dust and ruination and of the city beyond with its taste of stale waste and fuel. And then time breathes in.

With the same reverent yet destructive gestures we gradually remove each item of the other's clothing until we stand naked in the white moonlight from the skylight, our feet bare on the rough wood of the attic floor. She closes her eyes and I place my right hand on her left breast. She becomes whiter and whiter as I press my hand harder and harder against her skin. Slowly, surprisingly, my hand moves through and into her chest, without any blood flowing. She is still, eyes closed, as I find then slowly withdraw a living, sleeping bird from her chest cavity. I hold the bird in both hands – a dove or a wood-pigeon, stained with a little blood. Her chest is open. The bird springs to life, and like the books before it, I set it free into the starlit sky over our heads; the wind gasps.

I dress and carry her naked in my arms down the staircase to the garden, and she opens her eyes again a little, her face still very pale, saying *Won't you stay tonight? Why are you going to leave?*

I carry her out into the overgrown front garden. *Because I have to die again, or choose a death, it doesn't matter which, but choose it before it chooses me. Tomorrow nobody will recognise or remember me. There are always little changes, or I can take steps to make sure that there will be, put my face in the fire until I find a new face, and then everything will be different again ...*

I bend down next to the pond. She sits up a little and glances at her chest *... the wound ...* she says *... open again ... will it ever heal?* I run my fingertips over the tiny red edges of the slit between her breasts, seal it like an envelope and lean to kiss her. Then I lower her body into the cold still water. She floats just below the surface. I place my hand over her eyelids and close them, gather up the autumn leaves strewn around among the ivy, wet them in the pond and wrap them round her body until she is encased in dead leaves, in shades of red, gold, brown, and green. A dusting of moonlit frost now partially covers every frond and stem of ivy in a kind of skin. Perhaps the pond will freeze before daybreak.

I leave her there to catch a bus back into the heart of the city. I think I see a dim light emanating from the upper window where her father had spoken to me, but it might just be a trick of the moonlight.

The bus is late and empty: like a magical carriage for me, its only passenger. I don't like the driver's black moustache. He watches me on the back seat, in his mirror. Without the usual ballast of humankind the bus lurches and bumps. The driver checks my image in his mirror after each jolt, as if trying to impress or torment me. His moustache makes it difficult to see if he's laughing. Tired of this, I risk even more jolting by going upstairs. At the terminus, I come back down, but the driver has been replaced. *What happened to the other driver?* – I ask of the younger, clean-shaven man. *Him?* he grunts, pointing to the back of a uniformed man walking away, but he doesn't look the same either. I turn to step out, but he grunts again: *Hey, he left this for you … He said you left it here last night.* He hands me some folded papers. Confused, I accept them, and walk hesitantly, reading: *These are the notebooks of Ultrameta: city of the soul …*

I turn a page over: –

Something happened a year ago I never told you about. How could I? It affects not just us, but the entire fabric of the universe. My wife and I were in a car crash, or rather we weren't. I know what I saw. Suddenly we were going to die, but I was very calm. There were three cars, the one overtaking us was going to hit the oncoming one; the trajectories were mathematical, all three cars were marked for destruction. Time slowed down: maybe that's the first clue. Why does it slow down? Well, I'll tell you what it does next: most people don't live to find out …

Slowing down in mild fascination, I find I have just bumped into an old down-and-out leaning against a wall of the bus station. I pull myself together and walk more briskly towards a café. But, stopping at a junction, I can't help reading some more: –

Maybe we are never meant to know certain things because if we understood their implications we would go instantly mad. In the normal system of the world, we appear to live and die to order like helpless sheep, on the unknown whims of the unknown shepherd. But alone among all the things we observe in this world, there is one that never actually makes any sense: death itself. It is counter-intuitive. We know deep down that consciousness is inextinguishable. This is not a wish, but an unshakeable intuition. What if death were just an optical illusion?

I find an all-night café, push open the glass doors, enter and pull up a lonely perch. The barman pops up from below the counter, a dish-cloth in his hand, a toothless gap in his smile. I order a coffee and ask to borrow a pen. I test my handwriting on a napkin and compare it to the notes on these strange crumpled papers. They match up. I continue reading: –

At the point of death, or supposed death, time actually slows down then changes course to alter events. Nobody can experience death, so death is avoided, an alternative history is pulled out of the ether and dropped onto our plates. An infinite number of realities can be generated in order to divert death. When the cars crashed, they didn't crash: I saw them bend, pass through each other. I thought for a while that I might have imagined it, but days later, the universe began throwing me a few clues: a sunset sky looked obviously fake; every cloud identical, I would overhear total strangers saying my thoughts out loud on the train. Then I knew I was dead, that we all are, and trapped in a game ...

Leaning back in my seat, I feel I'm running out of time again. It must be four in the morning. I drink my coffee and smoke a cigarette, take a last look at this day's face in a fragment of public mirror. I scarcely feel I've got to know myself or the world, but maybe next time will be better. I like what I can see of the traces she's left on me, changes in my face. The eyes are tired as ever, the body ticking over, buoyed up by its electric shocks of contact, its rejuvenating acts of congress. This time I am too tired for electrocution and there are few cars around to contrive a collision with. I pay up, catch a lift to the 14th floor of a towerblock, break the lock to the plant room and stroll out onto the rooftop, scarcely pausing to admire the view. Same old city, though the blur of the lights at speed makes an interesting variation going down. I remember looking up at all the old books with their fluttering pages, and wonder if one of these times I might fly.

*

When I swallow this city, the sky walks into me. Always in autumn at dusk, when the day has finished everyone else. Again I begin, cocoon losing its butterfly, dying briefly – another death calling out my name. The sky is black turning blue, as if tainted, and the swishing cloth of coloured clouds turns my brow to that hemisphere above, wiping my eyes. Each day uses its end to my destruction – it opens me up so utterly ...

Inescapable city: your streets run to meet me, envelop me like a mother I have lost, or persistently forgotten. Familiar, unfamiliar. Every time, the fresh crop of faces, poison flowers turning to the sun, crowds of eyes welling with worries. They pass me by. Yet I am haunted by fragments, broken imprints of voices and features. I remember a girl, last night perhaps: was there a name? I was running my fingers along the smooth surface of her face, searching for clues, traces of my identity. Now, I think she may be dead.

Nothing. I remember only fragments. Being a child, sitting on a floor confronted by a mass of jigsaw pieces, my heart sinking at the prospect of re-assembling them into a picture. Later, as an adult, I might have solved that puzzle in half a minute, laughing. But this is all I feel now: a child's bewilderment, a blank sheet drifting closer to the mysterious centre of life, vanishing into a snowstorm of atoms, seeking new form.

Robin Fulton

What the Man Said

And God said: For God's sake give it a rest!
Yes I want you to keep looking for me
even when I'm not in for the minute.
Yes keep picking at the flimsy curtain
between life and death, behind which your friends
and relatives are beginning to crowd.
Yes keep winding your brain round enigmas
like: how a small grain of divinity
shrinking smaller and smaller can contain
more and more of a universe whose size
swells incomprehensibly hour by hour.

But after two-thirds of a century
can't you just take a day off now and then?
Your senses are still more or less intact
and your brothers and sisters have not yet
wrecked all the wonders of my creation.
Can't you watch a leaf opening without
going all epistemological
about leaves that opened before your birth
and leaves that will open after your death?
Even if God tells me, I said to God,
I'm not very good at doing what I'm told.

Above Dover Beach

Behind convolvulus and seeding grass
we park.
We see not one scuff or rip on the Strait
to show
two thousand years and more of heavy use.

Southward
across close-to-hand glitter and far-off
mauve haze
the other side if we believe our eyes
is not

there, just as we if we believe our eyes
are here
in a universe with a homely sky
and no
looming non-universes to scare it.

Below,
waves arrange the shingle, each with a crisp
cadence.
The tide coming in balances the tide
going out.

In the Dark

God said: Let the dark be dark.
Let the stars shine properly.
And let darkness with no stars
heal the damage caused by light.

Men said: Let there be light all
night through, where there is no-one
much or no-one at all, let
the gathered haze from street-lamps,
undying brand-names, full-blaze
unpopulated windows
stain the undersides of clouds
even when nights are cloudless.

God said: Light itself needs rest.
Some things are best seen, unseen,
in darkness unhindered by
Great Light. Me, for example.

Names I've Lost

Look like forget-me-nots bigger
than Scots pines. Look like sunflowers
but blue, smaller than heather-bells.
Look like fieldfares but they're scarlet
as they zoop into – not an oak,
leaves too lanky for Quercus – yet
it has many mansions from which
non-birds may safely be observed.

At night look like constellations
whose shapes someone described perhaps
to Homer. They do their best still
to seem two-dimensional, points
joined by lines which meet at angles
not even Cherubim could pull
out or push in by one degree.

Looking Up

No wall is as thick as this wall of rain.
In dense air a distant landing light seems
stationary, a confused star adrift
from its constellation, no name attached.

I look up from a page on which Borges
describes objects he can no longer see.

Roofs are so bright they darken clouds and streets,
tiles pay out light it must have taken them
years to save up. They spend it in seconds
as if convinced such light can never be lost.

Two Trees

Here's a public tree.
Like a fat post-bag
spilling its letters.
I wish it wasn't.
The year needs more time.

Here's a private tree
only five leaves, five
deaths. I shake that tree
to make it drop them
all five. But it won't.

Morning at Sea

In my dream no-one would listen to me.
But I had to listen to a dead voice
telling me: "That's both your parents gone now.
You've sat two exams. You were unprepared.
No-one will ever give you your results."

I lean on a bannister on Deck Six
watching how panorama window-panes
that slope in from the top make my image
– though faint – godlike and immune,
skimming deep water.

Reviews

Pamphleteer

Things are looking up for pamphlets, which are coming to the rescue of UK poetry publishing. Because of the increasing tendency of publishers to dispense with poetry as commercially unattractive, and of booksellers to be centrally-controlled, till-minded ... etc: everything conforms to specifications or goes unshelved. The Callum Macdonald Memorial Prize has encouraged publishers and writers to turn to pamphlets as a way out of the current *impasse*. Small presses like James Robertson's Kettilonia, Duncan Glen's Akros, Hamish Whyte's Mariscat and others are pioneering a new market.

There has also been a noticeable improvement in production, with the old notion that words are so holy that it matters not what the physical product looks like, and feels to handle. Essence Press (8 Craiglea Drive, Edinburgh) carry this to extremes in their superbly-crafted design by Julie Johnstone – their pamphlets look individually created, printed beautifully, with illustrations on transparent paper so you can see the poems simultaneously. One recent monograph is *in a sleeping cloud* by Malcolm Ritchie. The poetry is just as carefully laid out, sparingly with about 6-8 lines on each page.

in the still sky
the weather is hiding   (*big space follows*)

like a handle
on my own death

Essence publishes a magazine too: "*island* is a bi-annual literary magazine providing a distinctive space for new writing inspired by nature and exploring our place within the natural world". The press takes one poem by a writer, and then builds the individual book around that. Because the words are given such largess of space, we do have the opportunity to focus on them in a new way. An imaginative, different approach, and I certainly find the books and the magazine very attractive indeed. However, a previous pamphleteer columnist found the approach too precious, and the product so 'designed' that it became unhandleable. A matter of preference, I suppose – but a huge amount of care and love has gone into the creation of these.

Hansel Cooperative Press also take care with production and presentation: *Drops in Time's Ocean* by Christine de Luca, complete with the use of tasteful, grey endpapers, unusual in a saddle-stitched pamphlet, The pamphlet, refreshingly, isn't just a collection of poems, but the unravelling of a complex family history, the author's own. She starts with de Luca's great, great-grandfather, Alexander Pearson, and moving through six generations and a quarter of a millennium to her nephew, a Canadian, now 17. It's also the story of economic and social change for crofter/fishermen in Shetland – and much else, illustrated with photographs where available, and other relevant artefacts. The poems, most in Shetland dialect, except for the one in English to her nephew, more than live up to the vivid, skilful standard we have come to expect and enjoy from this writer. Copies from christinedeluca.co.uk.

Anne Scott too, cover apart, makes an effort to provide appropriate visual illustration to *Poems*, her privately-published pamphlet (from The Boat House, 34 (K) Charles Street, Largs). Her poems are extremely sensitive, well written, but more attention needs to be paid to structure – there are many places where the language could be tightened, and the line-endings re-examined. She also practices that old-fashioned habit of capitalising each line, which, mostly, only interrupts the flow of the poetic narrative. With Scott, as with other pamphlets to be considered later, there is a tendency to over-directness, and so the work reads as to some extent naive, but where an element of irony, or some objective 'mask' is provided, the poem leaps into more vibrant life. 'Poet Reading in Ireland, 1993', for example:

He looks as if he might dry tobacco
Under a sun somewhere yellow.
Gilded leaves of it
On his palms ...

The poems are accessible, and easily absorbed, but why, when she takes trouble to provide full colour illustrations, does she fall back on the title *Poems*, an entirely plain cover, and why, suddenly, does the typeface change to one inappropriately big? But it's good to see Scott looking to her own work – she has done a great deal in her teaching career for the cause of Scottish literature.

Poems from Kennals Cottages by Peter Isacke in many ways shares Scott's strengths and weaknesses. (United Press, www.united-press.co.uk) There is a tendency to the prosaic, though the writing is always fresh and competent, but I miss that tension and energy wrought through poetic compression. Most poems are a bit two-dimensional, failing to stir up deeper reverberations in the reader, though succeeding well on the surface. Initial caps at each line – again. Where irony breaks through, the landscape changes, as with the short poem, 'I Found a Head' –

Under an old, old wall
Whose skin was putrid, yellow, and cold.
And I wondered as the cool wind wasped,
What it had said that had so cropped
Its presence from the neck and shoulders.

It seems that the longer the poem being attempted, the less potent the result. Isacke's titles often intrigue – 'Wandering Near the White, White Cottage with the Tall, Tall Dog, Colour Poem' pricked interest, but the poem itself is bland, if enjoyable and well written.

Pikestaff Press (Ellon House, Harpford, Sidmouth, Devon) publish a number of pamphlets annually, and the standard of writing is generally high. In David Lightfoot's *The Pentecost Partnerships*, many of the poems share the above-mentioned limitation, but a couple of poems, again, the shorter ones, have genuine impact and bite. 'In those Barbaric Times' is quietly ironic about our treatment of people in death, contrasting the 'barbaric' treatment of the likes of William Wallace with that meted out to still-birthed babies of today. Similarly, in Robert Robert's 'Midwinter Power Cut', many of the poems are skilfully wrought, but don't reach that painful place. There are exceptions: 'Copy' describes a visit from an investigating journalist who clearly gets a bit of a hard time – the poem ends: "Keen news-hound or cold chronicler,/ He'll leave a dirty coffee cup". (Those initial caps again!) It is time, though, that Pikestaff brightened up its presentation. It looks as if it is created on an electronic typewriter that knows not the dash from the hyphen (dashes used throughout) and no energy is given to the cover design.

Kicking Lou's Arse by Alun Rees (Bucephalus Press, 67 Hady Crescent, Chesterfield) is an interesting failure as a pamphlet. Many of these poems are first-rate. He's got a wicked sense of humour and irony, and is a master of various poetic forms. Rees's animal poems show genuine insight into the nature(s) of the beast(s) – 'Snake' and 'Cats' are both vivid and thought-provoking. There are sparky squibs, sometimes on classical themes, like 'Building the Parthenon', briefly describing the sweat of the labourers, then concluding: "Then labourers toiled with picks and hods/ That poets might commune with gods", which should make all of us 'poets' go 'ouch'! The long 'Ballad of the Brave Captains' is admirably sustained through 140 lines of formal verse, and is followed by a series of 'Songs' (all fine pieces) to various occupations. The 'failure' comes in the concept of the book as a whole. At 60 pages, over-crammed with poetry, it needs a) a couple of blank pages, b) to be perfect-bound rather than saddle stitched – and be a 'proper' book of about 72 pp, with consideration given to the order and grouping of the poems. Or, it's crying out to be two, if not three, separate pamphlets, reflecting these groups. I'm going to tantalise you by *not* quoting Rees's wonderfully naughty parody of 'The Daffodils'. Buy the book – only £3.00.

Another publisher of pamphlets and a magazine is *Fras*, (The Atholl Browse

Bookshop, Blair Atholl – lovely name for a bookshop!) Prominent names on both its publishing list and in the magazine are those of its editors, John Herdman and Walter Perrie – absolutely nothing wrong with that! One fairly recent production is *Triptych* by John Herdman, three short stories, part of a longer work in progress. The longest story, 'Plaintiff' shows him at his weird and wonderful best. The unnamed narrator is reluctantly walking his wife's dog, Plaintiff. The dog disappears down a rabbit-hole never to be seen again (apart from his tail, that is, which puts in a guest appearance later). A little man with pointed ears turns up to convoy our narrator down the rabbit-hole to retrieve said dog, but the man finds himself in a strange world, Unplease (Alasdair Gray?) is an unholy amalgam of the Drunk Man's hillside (CMG turns up in the story playing the *Appassionata*), Alice's Wonderland, Tam Lyn's fairy-land, and goodness knows what else. One hobby in this universe is the torturing of postmodernists on an Ixiotic wheel!

This story, and the others, 'The Burning Curate', which combines heresy with a profane sense of the ridiculous, and 'The Owl of Soilluc', in which a rare owl is eaten by the protagonist, are written in Herdman's impeccable style. They explore situations and characters so bizarre that no-one else could possibly have dreamed them up, and make an extremely rib-and-mind-tickling experience.

The magazine *Fras* publishes accomplished writers, both new work and criticism/comment – and it sets high literary standards, but I do wish Herdman would exercise some restraint over his co-editor Walter Perrie's more splenetic outbursts, which leaves egg on the writer's (and the magazine's) face, not on that of his targets.

Mariscat (10 Bell Place, Edinburgh) publish *Passage/ An Pasaíte* by James McGonigal, deserving winner of the Deric Bolton Long Poem Award. Deric, now dead, was himself an exponent of the long poem, and gave great encouragement to us many years ago when compiling our *Long Poem* issue

(No 30). He turned to the long poem form because he wanted to deal with science, as MacDiarmid, Tom Scott and others have done. *Passage* traces the journey of the poet's ancestors (and, by implication, that of many other Irish 'immigrants' to Scotland) and the hardships they endured. In there too is poetic documentation of the lot of the miner, many of whom were Irish by origin. I'm reminded of Walter Perrie's *The Lamentation for the Children*, one of Perrie's most outstanding poems, published in the 70s, exploring his grandfather's mining background. McGonigal doesn't mince his words in his description of conditions, both the living conditions of the Irish in Scotland, and those of the miner.

> You are still in the dark. Let me say again
> it was soldier-like to enter the ingaun ee
> with lamp and pickaxe and descend
> with other men to be raised at dawn
> and cycle home. I was not alone.

The poem is expertly written, though I do have a number of caveats about it which I can't explore here. But its publication in pamphlet form underscores yet another value of this enterprise – the poem is too long to fit comfortably into most magazines. If, as seen elsewhere here, even work by Ian Rankin and Iain Banks is ignored by critics because it doesn't fit comfortably into acceptable categories, what chance does McGonigal have of receiving critical attention, except in places like this. The poem is a real achievement, and, like all good poetry, will open minds which remain open to vistas not yetseen.

Several pamphlets have resulted from the Stop-the-War Coalition, including *Celt A Arabica* by Ghazi Hussein and Jim Aitken. I am more than sympathetic to this, but have to register a reservation arising not just from these pamphlets, but long experience of editing *Chapman*. Being 'right on' with the politics does not in itself make for good poetry. Poems written in this spirit often end up being two-dimensional, leaving the craft of poetry languishing in the background. You have to be very cautious about poems written in the white heat of the aftermath of huge, emotive events like Dunblane, Diana's death, and 9/11. Poems have a life and vitality all their own, which often the poet has to struggle to reach. I do find this problem with some of the poems here, but clearly both Hussein and Aitken are to be taken seriously. I find their work succeeds best when there is some intervening idea, or structure, between the passions of the poet and the poem on the page. 'The War Orphan' works for that reason, and Hussein's 'Letter from Prison' is moving:

If you were to ask about me
Don't ask the sun
Ask the prison and its cell
For the answer is etched
In lashes that cover my body.

(Initial caps again!) Similarly, Aitken's 'Palestinian Immigrant' works, written with Ghazi himself in mind:

You can see the pain in his face
when conversation starts to fall
when his eyes seem to smart with sand
as if blown in from the desert.

But the design is a Bosch-like nightmare, each page emblazoned above and around with a pattern blaze, names are needlessly repeated, and it's set in an italic nobody could read with ease. There comes a point where good intentions don't make good poetry, or good books. With the best 'engaged' poetry, the content is lifted out of its original springs into a new realm, but here that final process hasn't happened. But there's no reason why it shouldn't – it wouldn't spoil 'the message', but, on the contrary, increase its impact.

Finally, a lovely effort: *Bioraacga Beag* agus *Biorachan Mòr* – a collaboration of words, poems, and translations between Douglas Beck, Derrick McClure and (pictures by) Màiri Kidd, published by 'Meanbh-Chuileag, 128 Lasswade Road, Edinburgh. It's a thorough delight, the poems are lovely, ditto the illustrations – and it's *so* good to see Scots and Gaelic doing it together. Get it for your kids, even if you can't pronounce the Gaelic, or the Scots, for that matter! Have an ice-cream, a glass of orange juice, and enjoy.

Joy Hendry

Theatre Roundup, Spring 2006
Scottish Theatre Enters New Phase
New Bows, Strings and Funded Arrows?

In February, the non-building-based National Theatre of Scotland was launched with nine productions on the theme of *Home*. The sites were varied: a Shetland ferry, a Glasgow high-rise, an Aberdeen low-rise, a factory and a secret location in a Lothian wood. It was not in a theatre, but a transformed space, that Scots got their first NTS experience.

The Lothian production directed by Gill Robertson of Catherine Wheels was the only one specifically aimed at the young. With its attention to detail and engaging acting, the promenade dramatisation of *The Babes in the Wood* story entranced all and left audience members treasuring being there.

Not all were so successful. Edinburgh, for example, with its lampoon of First Minister's question time, rather lost its point being staged in the Queen's Hall, not the Scottish Parliament Chamber. But some gave audiences outside the Central Belt who don't often get to see modern, innovative theatre, productions that are bold and diverse. *Home* did manage to be an embracing launch and suggested interesting collaborations to come.

By early May, five more full-scale NTS productions opened including three world premières. First up, from the Workshop Project arm of NTS, was *Falling* by the Angus-based Poorboy and NTS. Against the background of Glasgow and its streets, railway and underground stations and a spit-new office in Atlantic Quay, Poorboy director Sandy Thomson and her team created magical moments in a promenade performance where the actors and audience moved through the evening crowds. The technical logistics of performing *Falling* amongst the dynamism of a functioning city and underground was precisely achieved.

The story is deliberately disjointed, a young man who may be Lucifer follows a bewitching young businesswoman. After him are the angels or the gang he used to be part of. It was uneven despite two strong central performances by Brian Ferguson and Carmen Pieraccini, supported by 14 Student actors from RSAMD and a number of settings where Poorboy, as in previous productions, successfully involved artists in creating projects. But some of the striking detail Poorboy is now noted for was missing. Much was made of the perfume of the woman but not a molecule of it did we breathe in. The script, dramaturged by Davey Anderson and written by Thomson varied in quality.

During a quasi-religious ceremony in front of a surface that had become altar-like, the audience moved up the wide stairs we had been witnessing from and were offered small individual cups of liquid by the some of the supporting cast as if we were taking part in a mock communion. After witnessing the white clad boys/fellow angels menacing the girl, the audience were moved into a blacked-out people-carrier and the boy closing the door said with bitter hatred to us, "You better pray – fuck all good it will do you."

I had problems with *Falling*'s cavalier use of religious iconography and power, and came away feeling rather battered by these particular moments. It is one of just a handful of times in the theatre I have felt put into a compromising position. The problem with this is that you as an audience member start to be alert to the possibility that the creators' agenda is 'anti' people like you – which stops you being immersed in the drama.

Next came a co-direction by Vicky Featherstone, Artistic Director of NTS, and Julian Crouch, exceptional designer of the English theatre company Improbable, famed for their devised work. Co-produced by these companies it took writer Neil Gaiman's and graphic designer Dave McKean's popular illustrated book for children and devised, with the cast and other actors, a dramatisation for the stage billed as a *Musical Pandemonium*.

It's a surreal story in which a little girl hears wolves in the walls of her house and tries to tell her jam-making mother, tuba-playing father and gaming-addict brother.

They say they can't hear them and tell her, "when wolves come out of the walls it's all over". Playing the family Iain Johnstone, Cora Bissett, Frances Thorburn and Ryan Fletcher gave zesty performances, Johnstone playing a mean tuba but vocally closer to Rex Harrison – a technique that worked.

The wolves were curiously misshapen, hessian beings, designed to give a *frisson* to, rather than frighten, the weans. It entertained the over-sevens, their accompaniers and people of all ages who follow the cult graphic novel team of Gaiman and McKean, renowned for their many-volumed Sandman series. Due to tour the US later in the year and going to London for three weeks after opening in Scotland this production has an ambitious reach geographically and demographically.

The last of the three NTS spring premières, *Roam*, was performed on the way to, and in, Edinburgh Airport. It started with the theatre ticket, presented in a *Roam* airline ticket folder and then our bus was called in the Traverse bar. Checking that we all had our passports, for the performance went airside (where usually only actual passengers go), we then were driven to the airport. There we checked in as the performance continued around us leading us through to the departure lounge and back through a passport control and ending up at the baggage carousel.

Woven into *Roam* were choreographed moments and several stories arrived, left and then reappeared later on. In addition to celebrity arrival, the swinging pensioners off for a hol, and the mother with her hard-to-control children there was the acutely-honed drama of people trying to escape a civil-war-torn Scotland for safe havens like Sarajevo, Beirut and Kigali. In one strand, several people give us an insight into who they were, generations-here-Scot, Russian-ancestors-Scot or a person from the Iberian peninsular who has no country for her nationality. The show really brought home how varied and fascinating are the modern Scots.

The production soared and dived taking us to many different emotional destinations with Philip Pinksy's soundscape and Roma and South American music. Specially designed *Roam* branding and slogans including "we travel too much", held-up signs looking for 'Marcel Proust', 'Gravity' and 'Love', azure blue Roam uniforms, evidence of angels, quirky announcements and videos of civil war were just a taste of the production's rich texture. Andrew Clark, Itxaso Moreno and John Kazek were among the eight-strong professional cast which also included the powerful Saseen Kawzally. He was chillingly convincing as the military official eclectically deciding who got the last few places to safety. Director Ben Harrison brought great heart to this production, using the community cast imaginatively, to create powerful cameo moments for the audience.

It was like being transported to a brighter, sometimes entrancing world, conjuring up the romance as well as the present-day excess of flight. A serendipitous delight was watching the accidental theatre happening around us as Edinburgh Airport's last few evening flights landed and departed, with the amazed and amused real passengers stopping in their tracks to watch, interest and smile replacing their frowns and tiredness.

It is possible that every now and then, even with generous funding, NTS will not manage to pull off top notch productions of new work but they have started with a more than respectable first clutch.

The other companies have also mounted productions little and large worth noting. The Royal Lyceum presented John Clifford's adaptation of Goethe's *Faust*, both parts, text published by Nick Hern. Directed by Mark Thomson. Clifford's text, with its superbly crafted lines and fore-grounding of the writer played by a man and then a woman, provoked mirth as well as the unease from our own transgressions. Francis O'Connor's set used for both parts was another of his moveable circular creations. It changed as the books of Faust's study fell dramatically to reveal a structure where the characters could writhe and moving down and across close to the stage. He also introduced a mini-stage for some interior scenes. Later this was pushed away to the back, as though the red-suited Mephistopheles, seductively played by Dugald Bruce Lockhart, was falling down through the universe.

Producer David Maclennan's enterprise, A Play, A Pie and A Pint, had a fine spring season with some writers showing increasing ability with the less-than-one hour lunch theatre format and space at Oran Mor. It's also the company that offers most opportunities to established playwrights, established writers of other genres and new writers in Scotland. Interestingly it is sponsored by Orange and the *Evening Times* but the Scottish Arts Council do not supply funding. The fiftieth play since it started in Autumn 2004, *Nighthawks,* was a musical theatre delight, written and directed by John Bett with the music composed by Robert Pettigrew.

Set as the US entered the Second World War, Bett took the well-known painting by Edward Hopper and gave the four characters' lives. The result was sharp and witty political theatre – the lines all lyrics of songs. Bett showed himself very able in advancing plot in sung conversations and Pettigrew created tunes ranging across jazz and show tunes as well as a haunting love song for John Jack's Joey, aspiring opera singer in love with a man. Other key solos were George Drennan's Irish barman's song of exile and European refugee Lucy Paterson's Chloe's heart-moving 'Why Do They Hate Us'.

Across at the Traverse, once the only centre for new writing in Scotland, two new plays, *Melody* by the established Douglas Maxwell, published by Oberon Books, and *Gorgeous Avatar*, published by Nick Hern Books by new playwright Jules Horne comprised their spring season. Both plays, like too many from this theatre recently, focused on modern small town or rural Scots *angst*, both had a cast of four with the watchable Una McLean in both.

Producing five or six plays a year, the Traverse output looks puny compared to

Maclennan's. We are told the Traverse has more plays than it can put on, sad then they could not manage more contrasting and adventurous plays. Hopefully with their increased funding will come a rethink and an acknowledgement that a range of cast sizes and themes is needed. If this is what Traverse commissioned playwrights write, they should find others with different visions and sensibilities to put some surprise into the mix.

Diverse approaches to presenting theatre to audiences is important, different work too may draw a variety of audiences from those interested in innovative productions to those wanting to be entertained royally. Recent SAC decisions emphasising support of artists and viewing negatively audience-focused companies are very concerning.

In the performing arts, a work is not complete, indeed does not reach its ultimate realisation if audiences are not involved and engaged. An artistic funding body needs not only to ensure performing companies enable artistic development, but create and carry their audiences with them as they do so. All performing artists need to be aware of their audiences, after all, public funding is supplied by us, the people of Scotland.

There are many small lottery and other public funded, renovated and new build venues in Scotland relying on enough of a variety of highly active Scottish touring companies. These venues are too small and far-flung to attract commercial companies and if there are not enough subsidised companies they will be dark too often and the local audiences will be under-served because the venue's coffers are not boosted by box office income.

In the long term the SAC decision endangers the futures of these publicly funded Arts Centres and the possibilities of new companies arising and becoming the NTS's future practitioners or the Grid Irons and Poorboys of the future. The NTS looks as though it has many strings to its bows, let's hope that the funding of Scottish Theatre companies and artists ensure lots of arrows fly in the future.

Thelma Good

Catalogue 108

Anthologies have an ambivalent reputation, at least in the world of literature. Seen by some as a half-hearted sop to the general audience, but by others as a crucial stepping-stone into an unattractive and impregnable artform, they are both lambasted and lauded.

Being Alive (Bloodaxe, £10.95), sequel to the now-famous anthology *Staying Alive*, has had plenty of lauding. The original garnered critical acclaim and so editor Neil Astley came up with a second instalment. Like the first, this book is "poems that touch the heart, stir the mind and fire the spirit". So we get a run-through of most 20th century poets, and poems framed around themes including family, romance, and urban living. Especially welcome is the translations – a flick through produces Serbian, Polish and Greek – a reminder that poetry is not confined to Anglos only. The cover blurb (from Meryl Streep) (!) doesn't do it any favours, "this book feels more alive – I think it has a heartbeat"."

Another volume squarely-aimed at a market is *Handfast: Scottish Poems for Weddings and Affirmations* (SPL/Polygon, £7.99), running the gamut from Robert Burns to Carol Ann Duffy. It's an engrossing volume, though the topic in hand may weary those not aisle-bound. To choose just two, Christine de Luca's 'Journey' is quietly spellbinding with 'May you find bliss in ordinariness/ and joy forever in its present tense', and in 'Love Poem', Iain Crichton Smith cultivates a wondrously beautiful bleakness, although this may well put a downer on the nuptials.

Also beautifully produced and for lovers everywhere is *Chinese Love Poetry* (British Museum Press, £9.99). With gorgeous illustrations from the museum's collections, it's a delight to the eye, many poems serving as a useful counterpoint to largely western declarations of love. There's much to engage with, some of it surprising – 'a chaste wife will die with her husband' has a nice sentiment about it, though with a whiff of sexism.

Memory is a powerful thing, and in *The Collected Works of Lorna Moon* (Black &

White, £9.99) it exerts a powerful hold. Her early life in Strichen, Aberdeenshire provided her with a rich variety of events and personalities in small town life. Unsurprisingly for a woman who ran off to Hollywood, themes of escape and small-mindedness abound, but there's warmth for the close-knit community too. She might well have returned, had she not died in 1930.

Margaret Tait was also involved in film, although she came from the opposite end of the spectrum, coming from Orkney and distinctly non-Holywood. Combining short films with poems and short stories, she saw film as just part of her expression, and *Subjects and Sequences* (Lux, www.lux.org.uk/margarettait £10.00) does justice to her legacy with critical essays on her work, alongside poems, stories and her own thoughts. With its many superb images, this is a great testament to Tait's work and proves that film is a viable way for an artist to express themselves. It's a pity we only get stills of the films – a DVD would have been a natural extra?

The Thin Red Line (NMS, £12.99) might seem a bit of bellicose nostalgia, but it presents a more nuanced picture. The cover of the 93rd Highlanders in the thick of battle doesn't do it any favours, but there is much besides florid descriptions of imperial derring-do. There's coverage of the Scottish soldiers/sailors-of-fortune – Sir Samuel Greig, Grand Admiral of Russia, the anti-nuclear movement, visits of exiled Poles and Norwegians, the role of women and much else. We might be ashamed of Scotland's role, but the introduction wisely concludes: "Scotland's relationship with war should be recorded and commemorated, not because war is good or glorious, but because it is important".

Like a rather grand clock, Edinburgh University Press dutifully chimes out the latest volumes in its James Hogg series, this time *The Queen's Wake* and *Altrive Tales* (both £9.99). Although an epic poem about Mary, Queen of Scots' return to Scotland might sound grim, in *The Queen's Wake* Hogg manages to turn that besom with a fabulously bad

taste in men into something approaching a heroine, as poets and bards serenade her return. Publishing both the raw first and polished fifth versions gives an engaging comparison, giving insight both into the poem, and into the development of Hogg from a relative unknown to one of most famous poets of the time. *Altrive Tales* came near the end of his literary output, when his reputation was established. It falls into the category of unfinished works, this being volume I of a projected multi-volume series cut short by his death. But here is mastery in the short story.

In more realist manner, is *The Transformation of Scotland* (EUP, £17.95), edited by T M Devine *et al.* Tracing economic development from the Act of Union, it embraces everything from the development of a modern financial network, to the recognition of varying economies within Scotland. While the graphs and barcharts may trigger dusty memories of high school maths, there is much of value here, written in accessible language

An excellent primer for newcomers and a welcome reminder for old hands, *Modernism and Nationalism* (ASLS, £12.50) spread its net wide as its charts the growth of the Scottish Renaissance as it happened. There's of course the infamous spat between MacDiarmid and Muir, and much else: there's a chapter on women, coverage of urban and Highland poverty, connections with Ireland and the interplay between socialism, communism and nationalism in Scotland. Heartfelt thanks to editor Margery Palmer McCulloch.

On more learned ground is *Beyond Scotland* (Rodopi, $70) with weighty articles re-evaluating the Scottish Renaissance, the need for repression in creating a distinctive Scottish literature *et al.* Alexander Mackay's essay on MacDiarmid's relationship with the USSR deserves considered reading, though MacDiarmid's assertion about the mass-murder in the USSR: "even if the figures are accurate, the killings are a mere bagatelle … the Russian intervention was not only justified, but imperative" doesn't sound clever whichever way you frame it.

There must be something in the water: *Modern Scottish Culture* (EUP, £15.99) is Michael Gardiner's sprightly canter through this potential minefield. Though aimed at a young audience, this will appeal to anyone whose judgments could undergo a good shaking. He argues against writing in 'genres'; celebrates the interplay between folk, classical and rock music; writes clearly about Scottish philosophy as well as education and general cultural history. The tone might be a little basic, but he always writes with lively tone, coming up with some invigorating *bon mots*. In voting for devolution, 'The Scottish people's only mistake was forgetting that all parliaments are run by politicians.' Amen.

Two books portraying very different, yet oddly allied areas: *John Bellany* by John McEwen (Mainstream, £35.00) and David Johnson's *Scottish Fiddle Music in the Eighteenth Century* (Mercat, £20.00). McEwen's book details the life and work of possibly Scotland's most famous artist after Mr J Vettriano. The book has lavish, often spectacular, reproductions are always engrossing – the work after he visited Buchenwald stands out for its stark horror. McEwen's fluid prose is always overshadowed by the drama in paint. Johnson's book with its pages of notation, by contrast, will only come alive with a fiddler nearby. However, learned notes and essays on the development of fiddle-playing should inform those whose musical career began and ended with a kazoo.

As befits an outfit with socialist roots, Pluto Press has a history of publishing progressive critiques of the world. With *Marx and Other Four-Letter Words* and *Bad Marxism* (both £15.99) it has gone back to the master. *Marx and Other Four-Letter Words* is the more immediately readable, with many clear-sighted essays ranging from imperialism to division of labour – Keith Faulks' essay on capitalism deserves mention. John Hutnyk's *Bad Marxism*, however, gives off the air of a score-settling academic. Seemingly avoiding his own notions about applying the ideas of Marx to the real world,

Hutnyk uses academese by the ton (polyphonic heteroglossia, anyone?), which only enlightens the *illuminati*. Still, his turns of racy prose do compensate, and throw valuable light into a murky area.

Georóid Mac Lochlainn is an Angry Young Man in *Sruth Teangacha* (*Stream of Tongues*) (Cló Iar-Chonnachta, €15.00), certainly by the sound of 'Aistriúcháin' ('Translations'): 'Tired/ of self-satisfied monoglots who say/ – *It sounds lovely. I wish I had the Irish/ Don't you do translations?*' Elsewhere he explores the Troubles and growing up in Belfast with verve, though most will be reading the hated translations. For those fortunate enough to speak Scottish Gaelic, Martainn Mac an t-Saoir's *Ath-Aithne* (Úr Sgeul, £16.00) is an exquisitely produced 6-CD set of readings from his short story collection. Most are in Gaelic, but English-only speakers will get a flavour from the four English stories here. This is an excellent way of immersing yourself in another tongue.

J Derrick McClure's *Doric: The Dialect of North-East Scotland* (John Benjamins, €110.00) is a useful reminder of those who proudly define themselves against Gaelic, English and Lowland Scots. McClure shows with many examples of speeches, newspaper articles etc, that Doric enjoys a distinguished history as well as a lively present, describing the area in a way 'normal' Scots (let alone English) never could. McClure is right not to settle into cosy security about the language and righter still to see a future for Doric remaining as a living language. One dampener to this positive feeling is the series title: *Varieties of **English** Around the World*!

The trio *Goodbye Cruel World*, *Great Words of the Masters* and *A Book of Insult* (CRW, all £5.99) are stuffed with quotations – good for 'down' moments. The titles give a flavour of the contents, and with *bon mots* from all and sundry, there's something to tickle every few pages. A favourite is from *Goodbye Cruel World*, a list of memorial epitaphs: 'Gone to be an angle'. Misprints haunt us to the grave. *Edmund O'Connor*

Notes on Contributors

Peter Bromley: lives in Northumberland. When not looking after old buildings for a living, has had work published in a number of places, including *Route, Biscuit* and *The Echo Room*.

Belinda Cooke: teaches in Scotland. Her Russian translations have been widely published in journals and anthologies, with occasional sightings of Lesser Spotted Poems of her own.

Clare Crossman: born 1954, lived Cumbria till 2000, then moved to Cambridge. Shoestring Press recently published The Shell Notebook Poems about her Northern Irish family.

Ted Fink: a noted professional storyteller who can turn an everyday event into a spellbinding adventure. His original adventures, told in poetry and prose, explore the human condition.

Robin Fulton: has divided decades 50-50 between Scotland and Norway. Recent poems scattered widely in mags, turning up in Chinese, German, Hebrew, Spanish and Swedish.

Mark Gallacher: born 1967 Girvan, Ayrshire. Moved 1999 Denmark to live with Danish girlfriend. There first heard term 'sexual refugee'. One son, another soon. Published in UK, Italy and USA. www.markgallacher.dk

Owen Gallagher: from Gorbals; primary teacher in Southall, London. *Sat Guru Snowman* published Peterloo Poets, 2001. Awards from London Arts Board and Society of Authors.

Thelma Good: dyslexic writer of poems, short stories and plays. Theatre Editor and reviewer for www.edinburghguide.com.

Andrew Hamilton: born Greenock 1921. Now 85. Career in engineering with RR. MA and MPhil Glasgow Uni after retiring. Came to letters late, but isn't he doing well! Best genre fantasy – funny wee gremlins. No wonder he writes nonsense.

Angela Howard: lives France, writes poetry and prose, published UK and US small presses. Working on novel on First People's legends – epic adventure in semi-tropical forests of Mexico. Grandfather looked after Army mules, WW1.

Paula Jennings: featured poet at StAnza 2005. Hawthornden Fellowship 2003. SAC Writers' Bursaries 1999 and 2002. Poetry collection, *Singing Lucifer*, Onlywomen Press.

John Law: Citizen of the Scottish republic, general mover and shaker, editor of *Lallans* magazine, writes mainly for his desk drawer, from which a few items occasionally escape.

Morag McDowell: born Glasgow, educated Strathclyde. Now lives with family in a cattle-infested housing estate near Glasgow. Teaches Creative Writing. Winner/short-listed in competitions, including the Macallan, published in mags &c: *QWF, Cutting Teeth, NWS*, and *Mslexia*.

Alan McMunnigall: born in Glasgow and grew up in the Sighthill scheme in the north of the city. He studied at The University of Iowa and has recently completed work on his first novel.

Neil Mac Neil: widely published, UK & overseas. Four-poem sequence with artist for British Watercolour Road Show. Poetry, editing, reviews. Born Greenock. Now lives in Spain.

John Purser: publications include three books of poetry, *The Literary Works of Jack B Yeats, Scotland's Music* for which he won McVitie's Scottish Writer of the Year Award 1992. Recently completed critical biography of Erik Chisholm.

Edmund O'Connor: *Chapman* Asst Ed has two degrees and an uncontrollable passion for crime fiction. Can't stop buying books, or riding his bicycle demonically around Edinburgh.

George Pryde: a retired stress engineer born Glasgow 1934, has had stories published in Scottish and American literary magazines. He has completed a short story collection and novel.

Peter Snow: poet, storyteller and teaches various things at the Rudolf Steiner School. He is married with two children and lives in Edinburgh.

Douglas Thompson: Lives in Glasgow. Short stories in *West Coast* and *Northwords*. Computer artist and animator. Jumped off storage heater aged 2 trying to fly, bewitched by magpie. Poems rejected by Joy Hendry since age 12.

Alice Walsh: born in Dublin, 1960, lives with her husband and two young children in Perth. She works for an environmental voluntary organisation and writes sporadically.

Jim C Wilson: poetry and prose widely published for over 20 years. Twice winner Scottish International Open Poetry Competition and Royal Literary Fund Fellow since 2001.

Lynne Wycherley: poetry explores light, love, landscape. Forthcoming collection *North-flight* (Shoestring) ranges from Great North Road of childhood to beyond Shetland. Runner-up 2004 Scottish International Open Poetry Competition.